James W. Moore's
Finding Bethlehem in the Midst of Bedlam

Brittany Sky

Abingdon Press
Nashville

Finding Bethlehem in the Midst of Bedlam: An Advent Study for Children
Copyright © 2013
Abingdon Press

No part of this work, except as specified on the reproducible pages, may be reproduced or transmitted in any form or by any means electronic or mechanical, including photocopying and recording, or by any information storage or retrieval system, except as may be expressly permitted by the 1976 Copyright Act or in writing from the publisher. Requests for permission should be addressed to Abingdon Press, 201 Eighth Avenue South, P.O. Box 801, Nashville, TN 37202; or e-mail permissions@umpublishing.org.

All Scripture quotations, unless noted otherwise, are from the Common English Bible. Copyright © 2011 by the Common English Bible. All rights reserved. Used by permission.
www.CommonEnglishBible.com

ISBN: 9781426769016

PACP01269240-01

Authors: James W. Moore and Brittany Sky
Editor: Daphna Flegal
Designer: Kellie Green
Cover Designer: Keely Moore
Photos on pages 7, 31, 33, 36, 43, 47, 60 by Ronald Benedict
Art on pages 13, 15, 25, 38, 61, 63 by Mike Sofka
Art on page 14 by Brenda Gilliam
Art on page 27 by Hannah Jennings
Art on page 49 by Jack Pullen
Art on pages 26, 37, 50, 62 by Shutterstock®

13 14 15 16 17 18 19 20 21 22—10 9 8 7 6 5 4 3 2 1

Printed in the USA

Contents

Schedule/All-Church Event 4

Session 1: Nazareth 5

Session 2: Bethlehem 17

Session 3: The Shepherds' Field 29

Session 4: The Shepherds' Adventure 41

Session 5: Share Our Findings 53

Schedule/All-Church Event

This multi-age, all-church Bible study program for Advent is centered in the book *Finding Bethlehem in the Midst of Bedlam* written by popular author James W. Moore. In this book, Moore invites us to consider the presence of Christ: "Christmas or confusion, Bethlehem or Bedlam: Which will you choose this year? The truth is, we don't have to choose because Christmas always happens right in the midst of our confusion. God breaks into our confusion and becomes known through Jesus Christ. Christmas and confusion: Weren't they intimately related at the first Christmas when Jesus was born? Sometimes we forget that. However, this book is about how Christ breaks into our chaos and confusion to bring Christmas and how Bethlehem always happens in the midst of bedlam."

Resources for the Churchwide Study

Adults
Finding Bethlehem in the Midst of Bedlam by James W. Moore

Youth
Finding Bethlehem in the Midst of Bedlam Program Resource for Youth by Mike Poteet

Children
Finding Bethlehem in the Midst of Bedlam: An Advent Study for Children by Brittany Sky

Finding Bethlehem: A Child's Activity Book for Christmas by Daphna Flegal

Schedule

Many churches have weeknight programs that include an evening meal; an intergenerational gathering time; and classes for children, youth, and adults. The following schedule illustrates one way to organize a weeknight program.

5:30pm	Meal
6:00pm	Intergenerational gathering introducing Bible characters and places for the lesson. This time may include skits, music, and prayers
6:30-7:45pm	Classes for children, youth, and adults

Churches may want to do the Advent study as a Sunday school program. This setting would be similar to the weeknight setting. The following schedule takes into account a shorter class time, which is the norm for Sunday morning programs.

10 minutes	Intergenerational gathering
45 minutes	Classes for children, youth, and adults

Churches may want to do the Advent study as a weekend retreat. This setting includes meals; an intergenerational gathering time; and classes for children, youth, and adults. It teaches all of the content in a condensed time frame.

Friday

5:30-6:00pm	Light dinner
6:00-6:30pm	Worship
6:30-8:00pm	Session 1

Saturday

8:30-9:30am	Worship
9:30-11:00am	Session 2
11:00-11:30am	Intergenerational gathering
11:30am-12:30pm	Lunch
12:30-2:00pm	Session 3
2:00-2:30pm	Intergenerational gathering
2:30-4:00pm	Session 4
4:00-5:30pm	Session 5
5:30-6:00pm	Closing worship

Choose a schedule that works best for your congregation and its existing Christian education programs.

1 Nazareth

Objectives

The children will:
- hear Luke 2:1-5;
- discover that the journey to find Bethlehem began in Nazareth with Mary and Joseph;
- prepare for the adventure of discovering Christ's light on Christmas.

Bible Story

Luke 2:1-5

Bible Verse

In those days Caesar Augustus declared that everyone throughout the empire should be enrolled in the tax lists. (Luke 2:1)

Focus for the Teacher

The Bible Verse

Our Scripture reading this session includes the account of Caesar Augustus's decree for a census of the Roman Empire. Caesar Augustus ruled Rome from 26 B.C.E. through 14 C.E. He used the census to tax the people of the empire. The taxes were used to fund his various land conquests, road projects, aqueducts, and other public works.

In order to register for the census, everyone was required to return home to the cities or towns where their families originated. Since Joseph's family was a part of the family of David, Joseph and Mary had to travel to Bethlehem—David's place of origin. Luke has included this information for theological reasons, and not necessarily for historical ones. The birth of Jesus in Bethlehem fulfills the prophecy spoken by Micah in Micah 5:2. Micah declares that the one who comes to rule Israel, the Messiah, will be born in Bethlehem.

Nazareth

Mary was a young woman from Nazareth, the place our journey to Bethlehem begins. Nazareth was a small hill-country village in Galilee. Nazareth is halfway between the Sea of Galilee and the Mediterranean Sea, and about three to four miles from a larger city called Sepphoris. Sepphoris was prosperous, and was known to be the largest city in Galilee. The people of Sepphoris lived in elegant homes and mansions. Many of the people of Nazareth, however, lived in caves or used caves as a part of their homes. It is believed that the people who lived in Nazareth were probably the workers and servants for the people in Sepphoris.

Finding Bethlehem

As we prepare for the long journey ahead let's remind our children of the good news of Christmas. "God meets us where we are. God breaks into our uproar, our busyness, our hectic pace, our darkness, and our confusion through the birth of Jesus in Bethlehem—Jesus, who we know as the King of kings, the light of the world, and the gracious, forgiving One who understands."
—James Moore

Begin the Journey

Be sure that adult leaders are waiting when the first child arrives. Greet and welcome each child. Get the child involved in an activity that interests him or her and introduces the theme for the session.

Ask: Who can tell me something about the Christmas story? *(Give time for the children to tell you what they know about Christmas.)*

Say: Today we'll begin a Christmas adventure! It begins in a small village called Nazareth. Many of the people of Nazareth lived in caves or used caves as a part of their homes. It's believed that the people who lived in Nazareth were probably the workers and servants for the people in a nearby city called Sepphoris. We'll meet a couple of very important people in Nazareth. They'll be going on our journey to find Bethlehem alongside of us.

Mary's Home in Nazareth

Say: During Bible times, women like Mary had many important jobs to do. They cooked, cleaned, took care of the children, and were in charge of teaching their children about God. Today we'll live like Mary.

Mary's Well

Before Class: Fill up the water play table. Set out large empty buckets.

Say: One of the things Mary probably had to do was to go to the well in the middle of Nazareth and draw water for her family. She would fill her jars with water from the well and carry them home. There she would use the water to do other chores.

Ask: What chores do you do with water? *(Give children an opportunity to answer.)*

Say: Mary would wash dishes, cook, and clean clothes in the water she brought home from the well.

★ Encourage the children to use measuring cups or pails to carry water from the water table, "Mary's Well," to the empty buckets.

★ Once the buckets have some water in them, the children can wash toy dishes or clean up the classroom.

★ Invite the children to clean the washcloths by wringing out the cloths in their buckets.

Supplies
water play table, buckets, measuring cups or pails, washcloths, toy dishes

Grind the Wheat

★ Pass out a bowl and rock to each child.

Say: One of the things the women did in Bible times was grind wheat into flour so they could bake bread. We are going to use a rock to grind wheat like they did.

★ Pour a small amount of wheat in each child's bowl.

★ Show the children how to grind the wheat by mashing it with the rocks. They should not be grinding hard enough to crack the bowls.

Supplies
bowls, rocks, wheat

Taking Care of the Children

Before Class: Set up a baby center with baby dolls, baby blankets, baby bottles, and other baby items.

Say: The women in Bible times took care of the children. They loved them, fed them, and bathed them. One of the most important things women did was teach their children about God.

Ask: Who teaches you about God?

Say: In our story today, Mary is preparing to have her baby, Jesus!

★ Encourage the children to take care of the babies. They can rock them, feed them, burp them, and read their favorite Bible stories to the babies.

Supplies
Bibles, Bible storybooks, baby dolls, baby blankets, baby bottles, other baby items

Basket Weaving

Say: Mary probably also wove baskets. People in the Bible used baskets for holding food, for rituals, and for other practical things. We are going to weave our own baskets.

★ Pass out a strawberry basket to each child.

★ Encourage the child to choose some ribbon, yarn, or fabric scraps for the basket.

★ Show the child how to weave the material in and out of the strawberry basket through the holes.

★ Invite the children to continue weaving until their baskets look finished to them.

Supplies
strawberry baskets, yarn, ribbon, fabric scraps

Embroidery

Say: Women also sewed and embroidered clothing. Embroidery is a way to decorate things by sewing pretty patterns on them. We're going to practice embroidery, just like Mary!

★ Pass out a marker, a small square of shelf liner, a yarn needle, and a long piece of yarn to each child.

★ Encourage the children to draw a simple shape onto their shelf paper. They will follow along the marker line while they sew.

Supplies
shelf liner (available at dollar stores), yarn, yarn needles, markers

Teaching Tip
For younger children, use lacing cards and yarn.

★ Show the children how to thread the needle with the yarn.

★ Help the children weave the yarn through the shelf paper.

★ Help the children tie the ends of the yarn into knots so the yarn will not unthread.

Joseph's Carpenter Shop in Nazareth

Say: Joseph was engaged to marry a young woman named Mary. He was a carpenter. In Bible times, carpenters could be woodworkers, stonemasons, or craftsmen. They built buildings, roofs, doors, door frames, and even the tools they used to build with! They also made cabinets, tables, locks, stools, chests, and benches. Today you get to experience what it might have been like to be a carpenter like Joseph.

Make a Set of Carpentry Tools

Before Class: Photocopy "Joseph's Tools" (**Reproducible 1a**) for each child.

Supplies
Reproducible 1a, crayons or makers, scissors, glue sticks

Say: Many of the tools from Bible times are very similar to the tools we use today. They used hammers, axes, drills, chisels, saws, and knives.

★ Encourage the children to color the tool set and tool pouch.

★ Help them cut out the tools and the pouch.

★ Invite them to glue their tools onto their pouches.

The Carpenter's Shop

Supplies
toy tools, blocks

★ Set up a "carpenter's shop" with blocks and toy tools.

Say: Joseph probably spent lots of time in his shop building. You can pretend to be Joseph in his carpenter shop.

★ Encourage the children to be creative in their building projects.

Who Has the Hammer?

Supplies
toy hammer

★ Have the children sit in a circle.

★ Choose one child to be Joseph. Have Joseph sit in the middle of the circle with his or her eyes closed. Joseph will count to ten while the remaining children pass a toy hammer behind their backs. Once Joseph gets to ten, the hammer stops moving and Joseph must guess who has it hidden behind her or his back.

★ Play the game until everyone has had a chance to be Joseph.

Find Bethlehem

Invite an adult or teenager to dress as and play the Roman Messenger for the following activity.

While the children are still involved in their Begin the Journey activities, the Roman Messenger arrives on the scene.

Roman Messenger: Attention! Attention! There has been a royal decree sent from Caesar Augustus that you all must hear! The great Caesar Augustus has declared that everyone throughout the Roman Empire should enroll in the tax lists. You must gather your families and head to the city your family is from, so you can be counted and taxed.

The Roman Messenger leaves the decree with you, the leader.

Say: Oh my! The Roman Messenger wants us all to travel to the places our families are from.

Ask: Where is your family from? *(Let the children respond.)*

Say: Joseph's family came from a town called Bethlehem. Joseph and Mary were going to have to make the long journey from Nazareth to Bethlehem. They had about ninety miles to travel. They didn't have cars or trains or planes. They had to travel by foot. That's a long journey to walk, especially for Mary. She was going to have baby Jesus at any moment!

Ask: How do you travel when you have a long journey to make? *(Give children time to answer.)* What are some things you pack to take with you on your journey? *(Let the children respond.)*

Say: We're going to get ready for the long journey from Nazareth to Bethlehem, just like Mary and Joseph.

Preparing for the Long Journey

Map Maker, Map Maker, Make Me a Map

Before Class: Photocopy the map **(Reproducible 1b)** for each child.

Ask: A map is an important tool for a long trip. Why would we need a map? *(Give children time to answer.)*

Say: We're going to use our map to help us plan out how to get from Nazareth to Bethlehem!

★ Help the children find Nazareth on their maps. Then help them find Bethlehem.

★ Encourage them to trace the line from Nazareth to Bethlehem.

★ Invite them to color their maps.

Supplies
Roman Messenger costume, a sheet of paper with this session's Bible verse on it ("In those days Caesar Augustus declared that everyone throughout the empire should be enrolled in the tax lists." Luke 2:1)

Supplies
Reproducible 1b, crayons or markers

Supplies
Reproducible 1d

God's Own

Before Class: Photocopy "God's Own" **(Reproducible 1d)** for each child.

- ★ Invite the children to join you in a circle where they will hear this session's story.
- ★ Teach the children the response to the story and the hand motions that go with it.
- ★ Have the children practice the signs and words until they feel comfortable with the refrain.
- ★ Read the story to the children, pausing to let them sing the refrain where it is indicated.

Pack the Donkey

Supplies
Reproducible 1c, scissors, two chairs, two baskets or bins, an article of clothing for each child to hold, tape

Before Class: Make two copies of the donkey **(Reproducible 1c)**. Cut out each donkey's face. (If you have a large class, make three copies and have three teams and three chairs.)

- ★ Divide the children into two relay teams.
- ★ Set out two chairs, one across the room from each team of children. The chairs should be facing away from the children.
- ★ Tape a donkey face to the back of each chair and set a basket on the seat of the chair.

Say: To get ready for our adventure, we need to pack and load up our donkeys. Let's see which team can get all of their clothing items into their donkey's basket first.

Teaching Tip
Encourage the teams to play fair. Help the children cheer on their team.

- ★ Play a few times to get the wiggles out.

Bible Verse

Supplies
Bibles, index cards, marker

Before Class: Write each word of the Bible verse onto a separate index card.

- ★ Invite the children to sit in a circle.
- ★ Hold open the Bible and read this session's Bible verse to the children: "In those days Caesar Augustus declared that everyone throughout the empire should be enrolled in the tax lists" (Luke 2:1).

Say: Let's practice our verse. Repeat after me: In those days *(pause)* Caesar Augustus *(pause)* declared that everyone *(pause)* throughout the empire *(pause)* should be enrolled *(pause)* in the tax lists *(pause)*.

- ★ Get out the Bible verse index cards.
- ★ Invite the children to help you put the Bible verse in order. They may use their Bibles to help them if they get stuck.

Stop at the Guestroom

Divide the children into small groups. You may organize the groups around age levels or separate them into readers and nonreaders. Keep the groups small, with a maximum number of ten children in each group. You may need to have more than one group of each type. Make sure you have enough volunteers to manage each group.

Teaching Tip
Decorate your small-group area like a Bible-times inn.

Young Children

Say: In our story God chose Mary and Joseph to be the parents for God's Son. About the time the baby was to be born, Caesar Augustus, the ruler of the people, issued a decree.

Ask: Who can tell me what a decree is? *(a message about a new law or rule)*

Say: Caesar wanted all the people to return to their hometowns so he could count them and tax them. That meant Mary and Joseph had to travel from Nazareth to Bethlehem.

Ask: How do you think Mary and Joseph felt when the Roman messenger announced they must go on a long journey? *(Give time for answers.)* Have any of you ever gone on a long trip? *(Give time for answers.)* How did you feel when you found out you were going on your trip? *(Give time for answers.)* What did you have to do to get ready to go? *(Give time for answers.)*

Say: We got ready for next session's trip by making a map and loading our supplies on the donkeys. Now we're going to make a lantern.

Make a Lantern

- ★ Give each child a jar and a piece of black construction paper.
- ★ Help the child cut the paper to fit the jar. It should be the same height and go around the whole jar.
- ★ Invite the children to draw stars onto their papers and then cut them out.
- ★ Gently glue a piece of tissue paper onto the back of the paper. Let it dry.
- ★ Wrap the paper around the jar (with the tissue paper facing in) and fasten it with a strip of tape.
- ★ Let each child turn on a tea light and place it in her or his jar.

Say: The people from our story had to pack lots of things for their trip. When they stopped each night, they needed light to see. They didn't have electricity so they relied on lanterns to provide light. The lanterns they used were made of clay and used oil to create a fire. These lanterns will help us on our travels.

Supplies
glass jars, black construction paper, scissors, pencils, tissue paper in different colors, glue, tape, battery-operated tea light candles

Older Children

Say: In our story God made a plan to send a baby boy to the earth to teach God's people how to love one another. God chose Mary and Joseph to be the parents for God's Son. About the time the baby was to be born, Caesar Augustus, the ruler of the people, issued a decree. Who can tell me what a decree is? *(a message about a new law or rule)* He wanted all of the people to return to their hometowns so he could count them and tax them. That meant Mary and Joseph had to travel from Nazareth to Bethlehem. Caesar Augustus didn't care if Mary was going to have the baby very soon, so they had to plan for their trip to find Bethlehem.

Ask: If you had been Mary or Joseph, how would you have felt when the Roman messenger announced everyone must go on long journeys back to their hometowns? Would you have been excited, frustrated, or maybe indifferent? *(Give time for answers.)* Have you ever experienced a time when you planned something, and something else interrupted your plans? *(Give time for answers.)* How did you feel when you had to change what you were doing? *(Give time for answers.)*

Say: Mary and Joseph were not anticipating having to make a long trip from Nazareth to Bethlehem. Mary was going to give birth to Jesus at any moment. Most women are not interested in walking ninety miles so close to their delivery date.

Ask: What do you think Mary and Joseph thought when the census came and changed their plans? *(Give time for answers.)*

Say: Next time we'll take the trip with Mary and Joseph. We have all of the things we need to go, except a lantern for the dark. We're going to make one now!

Make a Lantern

Before Class: The night before class, fill enough tin cans with water and freeze. The ice will ensure the kids' safety during the project.

★ During class, pass out a can to each child.

★ Help the children hammer holes into the cans. When they are finished, have them pour out the ice and melt water in a sink.

★ Wipe the inside of the cans dry.

★ Give each child a candle to turn on and put inside the lantern.

Say: The people from our story had to pack lots of things for their trip. When they stopped each night, they needed light to see. They didn't have electricity so they relied on lanterns to provide light. The lanterns they used were made of clay and used oil to create a fire. These lanterns will help us on our travels.

Supplies
nails, hammers, recycled tin cans, old towels or rags, battery-powered tea light candles

1a Joseph's Tools

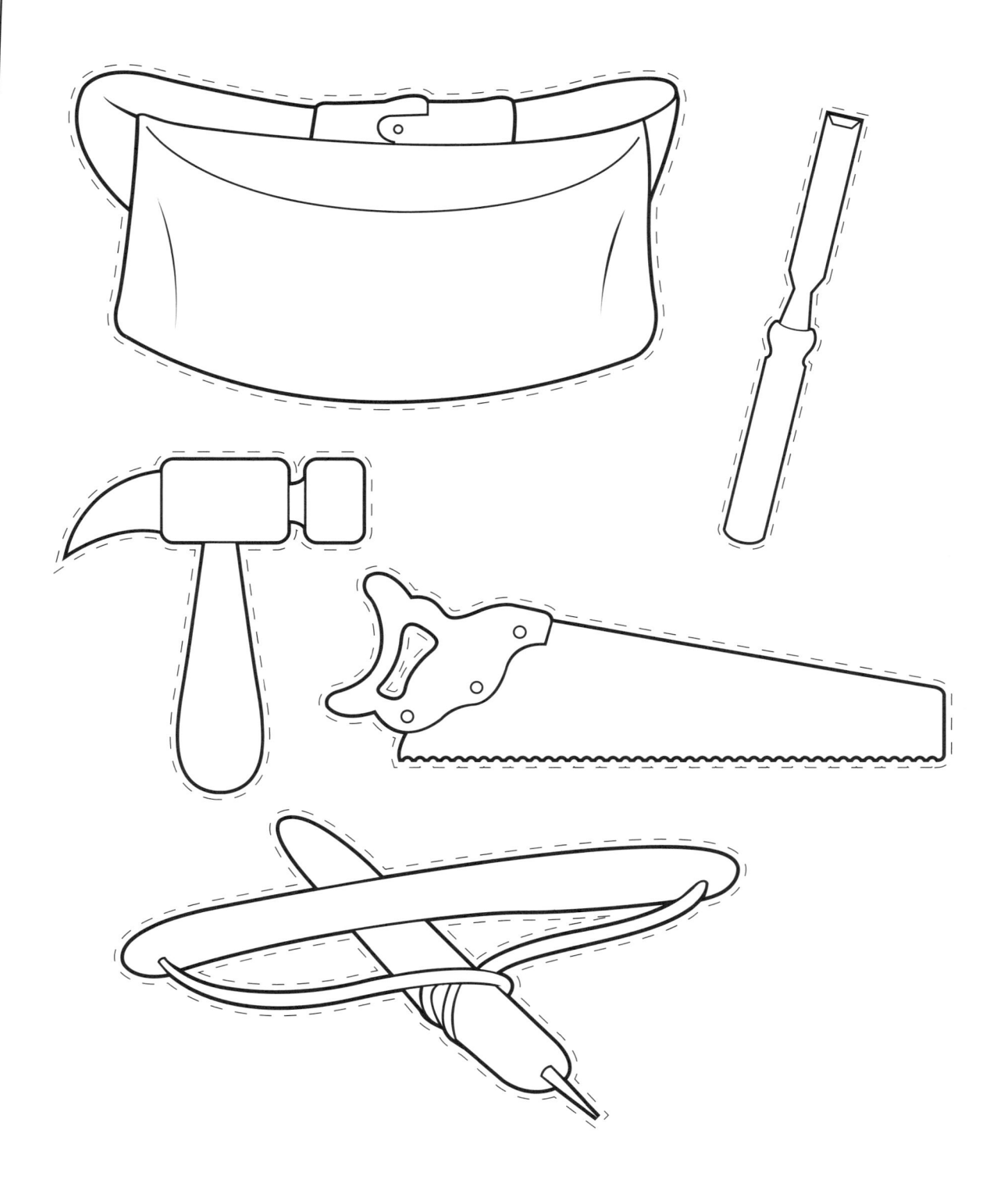

Permission is granted to duplicate this page for local church use only. © 2013 Abingdon Press.

Map

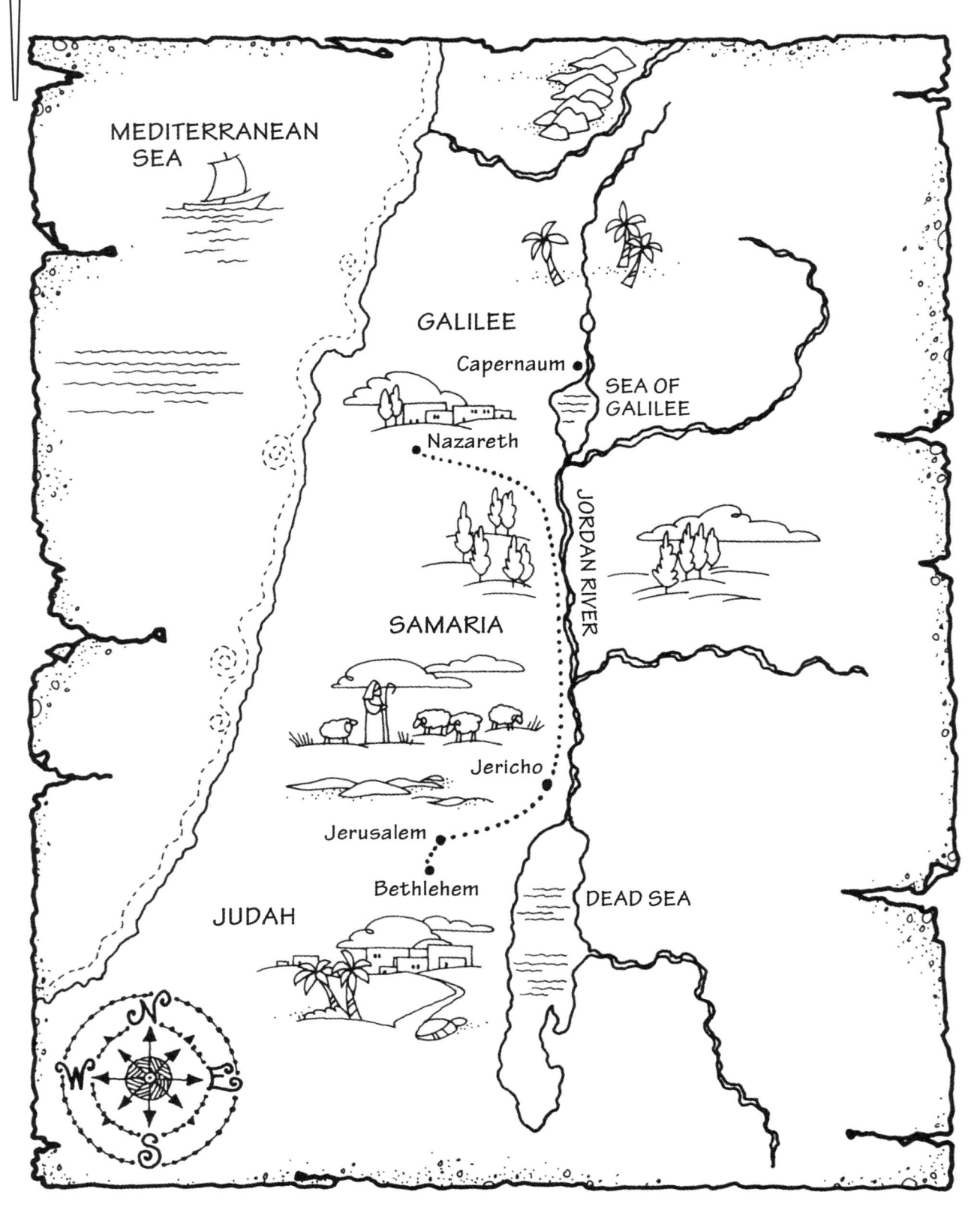

1b

MEDITERRANEAN SEA

GALILEE

Capernaum

SEA OF GALILEE

Nazareth

JORDAN RIVER

SAMARIA

Jericho

Jerusalem

Bethlehem

JUDAH

DEAD SEA

1c Donkey

1d God's Own by LeeDell Stickler

Teach the children the response to the story and the hand motions that go with it. The refrain is sung to the tune of "Little Cabin in the Woods." Have the children practice the signs and words until they feel comfortable with the refrain. Read the story to the children, pausing to let them sing the refrain where it is indicated.

Refrain

Little stable in the town
(Make a tent overhead with your hands, fingertips touching.)
Bright starlight is shining down.
(Hold both hands up, fingers outstretched. Wiggle fingers as you bring your arms down.)
Tiny baby, God's own Son
(Pretend to be rocking a baby.)
Jesus is the One.
(Touch the palm of your left hand with the middle finger of your right hand; touch the palm of your right hand with the middle finger of your left hand. Then hold up an index finger, indicating #1.)

God looked down at the earth. "I can't believe it! Even with the laws I have given them, they still haven't gotten it right. I've even sent my prophets, but the people ignore them. Nothing makes a difference. There is only one thing left to do. I'll send my Son. He'll teach them what they need to know. He'll show them how to love one another and care for one another. He'll set an example for them."

Sing refrain with motions.

"First I have to choose just the right family to care for my Son. I don't want the family to be too rich and powerful because then my Son will not know what it means to be just an ordinary boy. I want my Son to grow up like any normal boy and to learn to make his living, just like the rest must do."

Sing refrain with motions.

So God looked around and found the perfect place and the perfect family. God chose a young girl from the village of Nazareth. Her name was Mary. She was engaged to marry Joseph, a carpenter. And God said, "Mary will be a good mother for my Son. Joseph will watch out for her and for the child. They are just right."

Sing refrain with motions.

Then Caesar Augustus decreed that all men had to return to their hometowns to be counted for a census. Even though it was very close to the time for her baby to be born, Mary and Joseph got ready for a trip to find Bethlehem, Joseph's hometown. They gathered food, clothes, and things to help them on their long journey. They were prepared to continue God's adventure into this very world.

Sing refrain with motions.

Permission is granted to duplicate this page for local church use only. © 2013 Abingdon Press.

2 Bethlehem

Objectives
The children will:
- hear Luke 2:6-7;
- set out from Nazareth to busy Bethlehem where Jesus was born;
- continue the journey to discover Christ's light on Christmas.

Bible Story
Luke 2:6-7

Bible Verse
She gave birth to her firstborn child, a son, wrapped him snugly, and laid him in a manger, because there was no place for them in the guestroom. (Luke 2:7)

Focus for the Teacher

The Bible Verse
Last session we discovered that Joseph and Mary must return to Bethlehem, Joseph's hometown, because of the decree Caesar Augustus had issued forcing all people to return where they came from to be counted and taxed. They set out on their ten-day trip to find Bethlehem, only to find a busy, crowded town. Because of the hectic condition Bethlehem was in, Mary and Joseph could not find a place to stay. The only available place was a stable. No private houses, inns, or guestrooms had space for them. This did not stop God from entering our midst that day. Jesus was born there—in the hustle and bustle.

Bethlehem
During the time of this session's story, Bethlehem, a well-known town, had a population of five hundred to a thousand people. Bethlehem was about two hours—six miles—from Jerusalem. Bethlehem means "house of bread." The people there were laborers, shepherds, or farmers who grew wheat and barley. Because the grain was grown in Bethlehem, there were probably also people who worked in mills and bakeries.

Many Bible stories took place in Bethlehem, but the most famous was the story about David, the shepherd king. He was anointed King of Israel there, and Bethlehem became known as the City of David. Several years after David, Micah prophesied that the Messiah would come from Bethlehem, giving Israel another king like David.

Finding Bethlehem
"You were called to freedom, brothers and sisters; only don't let this freedom be an opportunity to indulge your selfish impulses, but serve each other through love. All the Law has been fulfilled in a single statement: *Love your neighbor as yourself.* But if you bite and devour each other, be careful that you don't get eaten up by each other!" (Galatians 5:13-15)

We must teach our children that we have the freedom to love because God deeply loves us. The story of Christ's birth reminds us of this great love. It is then our responsibility to share that great love with others. We can begin by sharing it with the children in our ministries. Through watching you love and care for them, they learn about this beautifully deep love from God.

Begin the Journey

Be sure that adult leaders are waiting when the first child arrives. Greet and welcome each child. Get the child involved in an activity that interests him or her and introduces the theme for the session.

Say: In the last session we met Mary and Joseph and experienced the town of Nazareth. We were forced to make travel preparations because Caesar Augustus issued a decree requiring everyone to return to their hometowns. Joseph's family was from Bethlehem, so he and Mary had to travel ninety miles from Nazareth to Bethlehem. This time, we'll head out on our adventure to find Bethlehem.

Travel from Nazareth to Bethlehem

Money for the Census Taxes

Supplies
Reproducible 2a, markers or crayons, scissors

Before Class: Photocopy "Herodian Coins" (**Reproducible 2a**) for each child.

★ Give each child a copy of "Herodian Coins."

★ Encourage the children to color the coins.

★ Help them cut out the coins.

Say: We'll need money for our trip. The decree says we'll be counted and taxed. We'll need to have some money to pay our taxes. Make sure to keep your money with you.

Traveling Snacks

Supplies
resealable storage bags, chocolate chips, raisins, cereal O's, pretzels, other trail mix ingredients you would like to add, bowls, spoons

Before Class: Check your children's allergy list before purchasing the snack ingredients.

★ Set out the different ingredients in separate bowls. Leave a spoon with each bowl so the children can serve themselves.

Say: We're taking a ten-day hike through the desert. Last time we made lanterns and maps for our journey, but we'll also need food. There aren't any places to stop and get food along the way. We're going to make some traveling snacks so we won't be hungry!

★ Give each child a resealable storage bag.

★ Invite the children to choose which ingredients they would like in their trail mixes.

★ Make sure they use the spoons to scoop the ingredients into their bags.

★ Save these snacks for Stop at the Guestroom.

We're Going on a Journey

Say: It's time to go to Bethlehem! Repeat after me!

"We're Going on a Journey"
(Tune of "We're Going on a Bear Hunt")

1. **We're going on a journey!**
   We're going on a journey!
   It's gonna be a fun one!
   It's gonna be a fun one!
   I'm excited! *I'm excited!*
   You ready? *You ready?*
   Let's go! *Let's go!*

2. **We've loaded up the donkey!**
   We've loaded up the donkey!
   With all of the things we need!
   With all of the things we need!
   Food and water!
   Food and water!
   Map and lights!
   Map and lights!
   Let's go! *Let's go!*

3. **We're headed to Bethlehem!**
   We're headed to Bethlehem!
   It's gonna be a long trip!
   It's gonna be a long trip!
   It takes ten days!
   It takes ten days!
   Let's go! *Let's go!*

4. **Clip! Clop! go the donkey's hooves.**
   Clip! Clop! go the donkey's hooves.
   Clip! Clop! We are almost there!
   Clip! Clop! We are almost there!
   Are you excited?
   Are you excited?
   Yes! Yes! *Yes! Yes!*

5. **We've made it to Bethlehem!**
   We've made it to Bethlehem!
   Is there a place to rest here?
   Is there a place to rest here?
   It is so busy! *It is so busy!*
   Let's see! *Let's see!*

Our Travels Painting

Say: Before we head into busy Bethlehem, we should stop and document what we saw along the way. We walked through lots of sand, through some grass, and by a few small trees.

Ask: What did you see on our trip?

★ Give each child a smock, a paintbrush, a paper plate, and a piece of heavy stock paper.

★ Invite the children to come to you for paint. Squirt a little of each color of paint onto their paper plates.

★ Encourage the children to paint what they saw along the way.

★ Invite the children to show their paintings to the class and explain what they saw on the journey.

★ Lay the paintings flat to dry.

Supplies
heavy stock paper, paints, paintbrushes, paper plates, smocks or aprons or old T-shirts

Find Bethlehem

Supplies
Bible-times costumes

Invite two adults or teenagers to dress as and play the Census Taker and the Tax Collector for the following activity.

Census Taker: Welcome to Bethlehem! This must be your hometown. Everyone in Bethlehem today must be added to the census. I'll need each of you to fill out a census form, and then you'll have to pay taxes to the Roman government.

Tax Collector: That's where I come in! You'll have to pay taxes so we can continue to build roads and sewage systems and make land purchases.

Census Taker: After you fill out the census form at your tables, please return them to me.

Tax Collector: Then line up in front of me. Make sure you have your coins handy!

O Little Town of Bethlehem

Added to the Census

Supplies
Reproducible 2b, crayons or markers

Before Class: Photocopy "Census Form" **(Reproducible 2b)** for each child.

★ Pass out a "Census Form" to each child.

Say: A census is used by a government to find out information about the people in their area. A census will usually ask how many people are in your family, how much money you make, what job you have, what your address is, and anything else that will help the government better know who is living in their region. We're going to fill out a census form about ourselves, just like Joseph and Mary would have had to do.

★ Help the children fill out their information on the census form.

★ Invite them to color their forms.

★ Give the forms to the Census Taker.

Pay Taxes

Supplies
coins made earlier, box with a slit in the lid to put coins in

★ Invite the children to gather the coins they made earlier in the lesson.

Say: Now that we have turned in our census forms, we must pay our taxes. Let's line up in front of the Tax Collector.

Tax Collector: Thank you for coming to pay your taxes! I'll need five coins from each of you.

★ Help the children count out five coins.

- ★ Encourage the children to place their coins inside the Tax Collector's box.

Say: Now that we have paid our taxes, let's check in with Joseph and Mary. They made the long trek to Bethlehem from Nazareth, too.

Bible Story

Before Class: Photocopy "The Trip to Bethlehem" **(Reproducible 2d)** for each actor. Recruit three adults or youth to act out the story.

- ★ Act out the story for the children.
- ★ Encourage the children to repeat "clip, clop, clip, clop, clip, clop" with the narrator.

Supplies
Reproducible 2d, Bible-times costumes

No Room

- ★ Create "inns" on the floor by taping different colors of construction paper to the floor.

Say: Now that we have registered in the census and paid our taxes, we should find a place to stay. Mary and Joseph couldn't find a room.

Ask: Do you think we will find a place to rest?

- ★ Invite all of the children to stand on an "inn."
- ★ Instruct them to move around from inn to inn when they hear Christmas music playing.
- ★ When the music stops, they have five seconds to get in an inn. If they can't find an inn in time, they must sit down.
- ★ After each round, remove one of the inns. Play until you have only one child left in the game.

Supplies
construction paper, masking tape, CD of Christmas music, CD player

Baby Jesus Is Born

Before Class: Split a walnut into two halves. Be careful not to crack the shell. One way to do this is to use a kitchen knife. Insert the knife into any weak spot on the shell, and give the knife a few taps until the walnut opens. Each child will need half a shell. Cut ribbon into four-inch pieces. Cut chenille stems in half.

Say: A very pregnant Mary and Joseph traveled all the way from Nazareth to Bethlehem to be counted in the Roman census. When they arrived there was no place for them to sleep. To make things more stressful, Mary was ready to have the baby! They found a stable to sleep in, and that is where Mary and Joseph had baby Jesus.

Supplies
walnut shells, ribbon, chenille stems, scissors, wooden beads, glue, fabric scraps, permanent markers

Teaching Tip
If you have a large group or a nut allergy, you can use an egg carton instead. Cut the carton into twelve pieces, so each child would have an egg-sized baby bed.

Supplies
Bible

- ★ Give each child a walnut half, a ribbon, a chenille stem, a wooden bead, glue, and two fabric scraps.
- ★ Invite the children to glue the ribbon onto the walnut shell so they can hang their baby in a manger on a Christmas tree.
- ★ Show them how to string the bead onto the chenille stem. The bead will be the head of baby Jesus, so leave the bead close to the end of the chenille stem.
- ★ Encourage them to wrap the long end of the chenille stem around their fingers. This will give baby Jesus a body.
- ★ Invite them to glue one fabric scrap on the inside of the walnut. Then, lay baby Jesus on top of this "blanket" and cover him with the other scrap of fabric.
- ★ Help each child draw a face onto the bead.

Bible Verse

- ★ Invite the children to sit in a circle.
- ★ Hold open the Bible and read this session's Bible verse to the children: "She gave birth to her firstborn child, a son, wrapped him snugly, and laid him in a manger, because there was no place for them in the guestroom" (Luke 2:7).

Say: Let's practice our verse. Repeat after me: She gave birth to (pause) her firstborn child, a son (pause), wrapped him snugly (pause), and laid him in a manger (pause), because no place (pause) for them in the guestroom (pause).

- ★ Invite the children to sing the Bible verse song to the tune of "We're Following the Leader" with you.

1. She had baby
   Jesus,
   Jesus,
   Jesus.
   She had baby
   Jesus,
   Her firstborn
   son.

2. She laid him in a
   manger,
   A manger,
   A manger.
   She laid him in a
   manger,
   No room in the
   inn.

3. She wrapped him
   so snugly,
   So snugly,
   So snugly.
   She wrapped him
   so snugly,
   To show him her
   love.

Stop at the Guestroom

Divide the children into small groups. You may organize the groups around age levels or separate them into readers and nonreaders. Keep the groups small, with a maximum number of ten children in each group. You may need to have more than one group of each type. Make sure you have enough volunteers to manage each group.

Young Children

Say: Whew! What a long journey we made! We traveled all the way from Nazareth to Bethlehem. Bethlehem was so busy that Mary and Joseph couldn't find anywhere to stay either. It's a good thing they found a stable to stay in for the night, and just in time, too! Baby Jesus came that night. The busyness and craziness did not stop him from entering our world. That is the most important thing to remember. Jesus came because God loves us, and no amount of hustle and bustle will ever keep Jesus from being in our lives.

Say: To help us remember about God's love for us that came through a baby named Jesus, we are going to make a Nativity poster to hang up in our homes. Every time we see it, we can remember that God's love is freely given to us through Jesus.

Make a Nativity Poster

Before Class: Photocopy "The Nativity" **(Reproducible 2c)** for each child.

★ Give each child "The Nativity." Encourage the children to color the manger scene.

★ Help each child cut the manger scene on the dotted line.

★ Invite the children to each glue the scene onto a piece of scrapbook paper.

★ Encourage the children to cut the Bible verse square out of the reproducible page and glue it underneath the manger scene.

Say: Our Bible verse says, "She gave birth to her firstborn child, a son, wrapped him snugly, and laid him in a manger, because there was no place for them in the guestroom" (Luke 2:7). I invite all of you to take this home with you and to hang the poster somewhere your whole family can see it to remind you and your family of God's love.

Supplies
Reproducible 2c, markers or crayons, scissors, scrapbook paper or construction paper, glue

Older Children

Say: Some biblical historians believe that there may have been as many as 1 million visitors trudging the streets of Bethlehem the night that Mary and Joseph arrived. That's a lot of people.

Ask: What do you think would happen if a million extra people showed up in our town? *(Give the children time to answer.)* What would that do to our roads and the lines at our stores? *(Give the children time to answer.)*

Say: We may never have experienced the chaos of what probably happened in Bethlehem when everyone came to be counted and taxed. What kinds of sounds do you think filled the air that night? Maybe donkey brays and lots of shouting.

Ask: What do you hear when you imagine the day Mary and Joseph arrived in Bethlehem? *(Let the children respond.)*

Say: That sounds busy! But the busyness, and the craziness, did not keep Jesus from being born. The busyness and craziness did not stop him from entering our world. That is the most important thing to remember. Jesus came because God loves us, and no amount of hustle and bustle will ever keep Jesus from being in our lives.

Say: To help us remember about God's love for us that came through a baby named Jesus, we are going to make a Nativity poster to hang up in our homes. Every time we see it, we can remember that God's love is freely given to us through Jesus.

Make a Nativity Poster

Before Class: Photocopy "The Nativity" **(Reproducible 2c)** for each child.

★ Give each child "The Nativity." Encourage the children to color the manger scene.

★ Have the children cut the manger scene on the dotted line.

★ Invite the children to glue the scene onto a piece of scrapbook paper.

★ Encourage the children to cut the Bible verse square out of the reproducible page and glue it underneath the manger scene.

Say: Our Bible verse says, "She gave birth to her firstborn child, a son, wrapped him snugly, and laid him in a manger, because there was no place for them in the guestroom" (Luke 2:7). I invite all of you to take this home with you and to hang the poster somewhere your whole family can see it.

Supplies
Reproducible 2c, markers or crayons, scissors, scrapbook paper or construction paper, glue

2a Herodian Coins

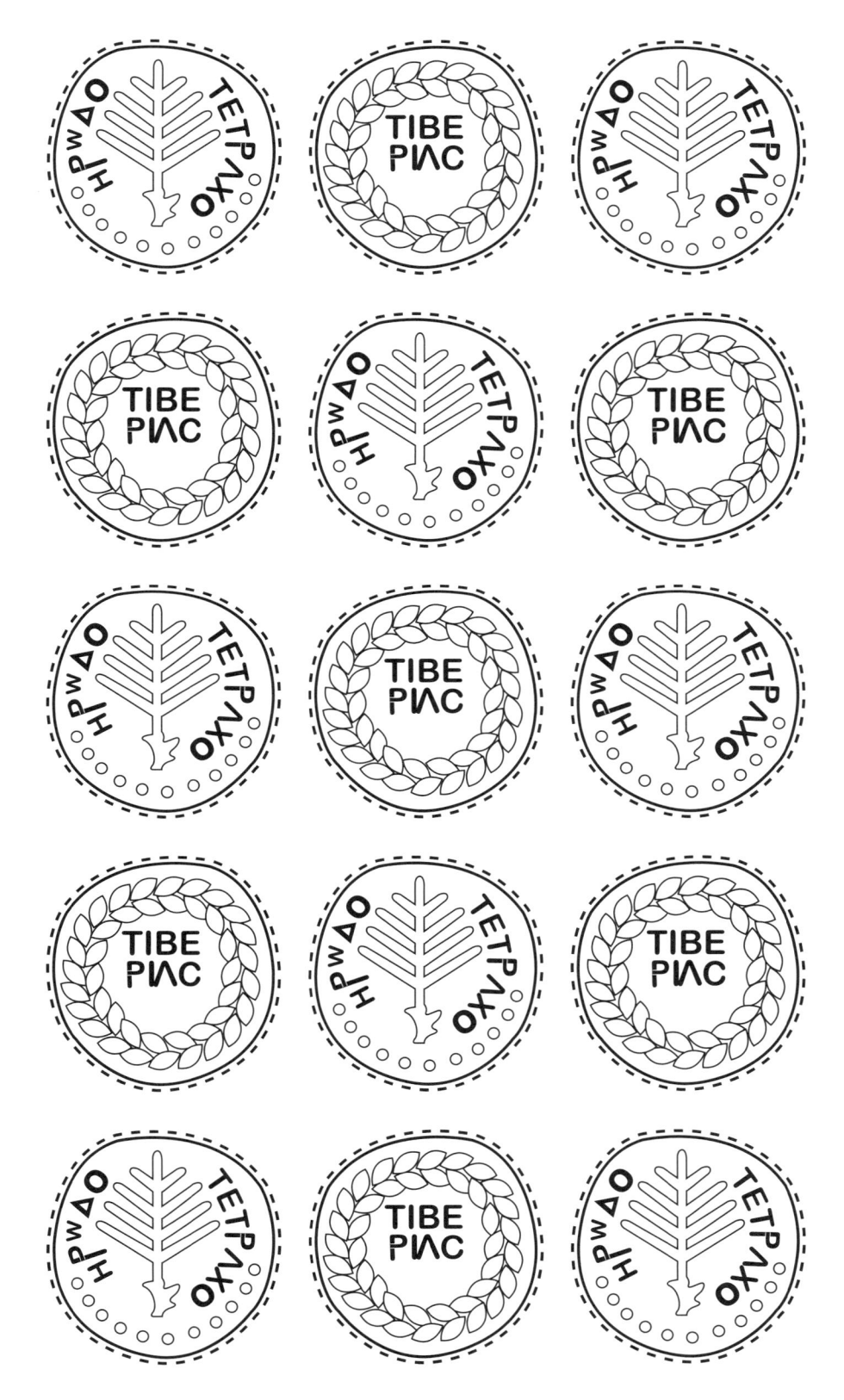

# Census Form

Roman Census

Name: _____

Birthday: _____

Hometown: _____

Names of family members:

_____

_____

Favorite Hobby:

_____

The Nativity

She gave birth to her firstborn child, a son, wrapped him snugly, and laid him in a manger, because there was no place for them in the guestroom. (Luke 2:7)

The Trip to Bethlehem

by Judy Newman-St. John

Characters: *Narrator, Joseph, and Mary*
Props: *chair (pretend donkey for Mary to sit on)*

Narrator: Mary and Joseph are on their way to Bethlehem to be registered. Mary is riding a donkey that clip-clops down the rocky dirt road.

Narrator: Clip, clop, clip, clop, clip, clop!

Joseph: *(to Mary)* How are you, Mary? Are you tired?

Mary: *(nods yes to Joseph)* Yes, I am. But I think you may be tired as well. Even our little donkey must be tired. He has carried me such a long way.

Narrator: Clip, clop, clip, clop, clip, clop!

Joseph: *(to himself)* Yes, I'm tired, and worried. I have more to worry about than paying taxes. I'm sure the Romans want to get every bit of money they can, but I'll register, and I'll pay my taxes. I just hope this trip isn't too hard on Mary. Her baby could come any minute! Hmmm. *Her* baby? *Our* baby!

Narrator: Joseph remembered back to when Mary told him about the angel who had spoken to her. She had felt God's Spirit, and she would have a baby, God's Son.

Joseph: *(to himself)* Yes, our baby. I know that he is the Son of God, and I'll be his father on earth. Mary and I will love him as much as any parents ever loved their baby. I'll be a good father. I'll teach him the Torah, and he will grow up to be a man of God. I'll teach him everything I know about woodworking.

Mary: *(Mary touches Joseph's arm.)* Joseph, I think I see the city in the distance! I'm so glad. I would like to get off this donkey!

Narrator: The journey to Bethlehem was not an easy one, especially for a woman about to have a baby. The little donkey did the best he could to make her trip comfortable. He stepped around rocks and over any rough spots in the road.

Narrator: Clip, clop, clip, clop, clip, clop!

Mary: *(to herself)* I know God will take care of us. God sent an angel to Joseph in a dream. The angel told him that my baby is God's beloved child. The angel told Joseph to marry me. And now we are on our way and our baby will be born soon. I'll be a good mother to our baby. I'll be sure that he is fed, warm, and happy. I'll take extra care to raise God's chosen child in the way God wants me to.

Mary: *(to Joseph)* I've been thinking about our baby. The angel told us to name him Jesus.

Joseph: *(to Mary, smiling)* I've been thinking of our baby also. I think Jesus is the perfect name for him. I've been wondering if he will look like you.

Mary: *(smiling)* He'll be beautiful, I know.

Narrator: The couple approached the busy, crowded city. Joseph made his way from place to place searching for somewhere to stay. The little donkey was careful that he did not bump into any person or other animal.

Narrator: Clip, clop, clip, clop, clip, clop!

Joseph: Mary, I must find a place for you to rest, but all of the rooms are full.

Narrator: One kind person offered their stable to Mary and Joseph. It was a place where animals slept, but they could rest there and be warm and dry. Once inside the stable, Joseph made Mary a bed of soft hay.

Joseph: *(to Mary)* Come, my love. Rest a while.

Mary: Yes, I will rest. Soon, very soon, our baby will be born.

Permission is granted to duplicate this page for local church use only. © 2013 Abingdon Press.

3 The Shepherds' Field

Objectives

The children will:
- ★ hear Luke 2:8-14;
- ★ meet the shepherds and the angels;
- ★ continue the journey to discover Christ's light on Christmas.

Bible Story

Luke 2:8-14

Bible Verse

Your savior is born today in David's city. He is Christ the Lord. (Luke 2:11)

Focus for the Teacher

The Bible Verse

Our story today involves two groups of people: a group of shepherds in a field near Bethlehem and a group of angelic messengers. Jesus, Christ the Lord, has just been born! That certainly deserves an announcement. The Scripture surprises readers, especially the first-century readers, when shepherds are the first to hear the announcement of the Messiah.

Shepherds

Shepherds in the first century were the lowest group on the totem pole. They were viewed by their society as shiftless, dishonest people who grazed their flocks on other people's land. The religious leaders in the Jewish community also looked down upon them. Because of the nature of their work, shepherds were not able to observe all of the religious laws. It was impossible for shepherds to follow all of the rules about detailed hand washing and food handling. Luke's mention of them in his Gospel account of the story does two things: further develops Jesus' connection with David and with Bethlehem, and shows Jesus being sent to the lowly and outcast.

Angels

The shepherds were watching their flocks this night, and then an angel of the Lord appeared to them. Luke does not give us a name or description of the angel, but the Bible tells us this angel was a messenger of God. The angel announces the Christ child born in Bethlehem and says that they will find him in a manger. Then more angels appear to the shepherds, praising God and proclaiming peace.

Finding Bethlehem

"Jesus responded, 'Go, report to John what you hear and see. Those who were blind are able to see. Those who were crippled are walking. People with skin diseases are cleansed. Those who were deaf now hear. Those who were dead are raised up. The poor have good news proclaimed to them'" (Matthew 11:4-5).

"This is the good news of Christmas, isn't it? Christ came to us in this world in the power of love. The Word of God became flesh and blood. The Word of God was wrapped up in a person named Jesus, who came and dwelt among us full of grace, full of truth, full of love."—James Moore

Begin the Journey

Be sure that adult leaders are waiting when the first child arrives. Greet and welcome each child. Get the child involved in an activity that interests him or her and introduces the theme for the session.

Say: Mary was nine months pregnant when Caesar Augustus decreed that everyone must travel to their hometowns to be counted in a census and taxed. Joseph's family was from Bethlehem, so he and Mary had to travel the ninety miles, which took ten days, to be counted. They got to a very busy Bethlehem and could not find a place to stay. They ended up in a stable just in time for Mary to have her baby. She wrapped her baby in snug cloth and laid him in a manger.

Say: Now we will venture to a nearby shepherds' field. The shepherds are in for an adventure!

A Nearby Shepherds' Field

Sheepscape

Supplies
green and dark blue construction paper, cotton balls, glue, scissors, black markers, star stickers

★ Give each child a piece of green construction paper, a piece of blue construction paper, and several cotton balls.

★ Show the children how to cut the green paper to look like hills and then glue the green hills to the blue paper.

★ Encourage the children to glue cotton balls on the hillside.

★ Invite them to use a black marker to draw four legs and a head around each cotton ball to make it look like a sheep.

★ Invite them to add star stickers to the blue sky.

Say: We're going to visit a sheep field near Bethlehem. The shepherds there will go on an adventure themselves!

Hide and Sheep

★ Choose one child to be the Shepherd.

★ Let the rest of the children (the sheep) find hiding places.

★ The Shepherd will count to ten and then try to find the sheep. (The sheep can make sheep sounds while they hide.)

★ Play the game a few times so everyone who wants to be the Shepherd has an opportunity to do so.

Say: The shepherds looked after the sheep. They kept the sheep safe and took care of the things the sheep needed. There isn't much grass around Bethlehem, so each day they moved the sheep around so the sheep could graze on grass.

Build a Sheepfold

Say: The shepherds would move the sheep to a place called a sheepfold at night. The sheepfold was a way to keep the sheep safe from predators. The sheep couldn't get out, and the predators couldn't get in. The shepherds would sleep right beside the sheepfold so they could keep the sheep safe.

★ Encourage the children to use blocks or boxes to build a sheepfold.

★ Invite them to herd the sheep figures or stuffed animals into the sheepfold.

★ Let the children lie down outside of the sheepfold and pretend to sleep under the stars next to the sheep.

Supplies
blocks or small boxes, sheep figures or stuffed animals

Wolf and Sheep Tag

Say: Shepherds took good care of their sheep. They did their best to keep them safe from all harm.

★ Separate the children into groups of four.

★ Each group will need a wolf, a sheep, and two shepherds. The sheep joins hands with the shepherds, forming a three-person triangle.

★ The wolf, standing outside the group, tries to tag the sheep while the shepherds (without breaking their circle of hands) spin around, trying to keep the wolf at bay.

★ When the wolf tags the sheep, the players change roles and play again.

Black Sheep Bubble Painting

Before Class: Mix liquid soap with water and black tempera paint.

★ Give each child a straw and a piece of white paper.

★ Invite the children to dip their straws into the soap and paint mixture and then blow bubbles onto their papers.

★ Set the papers aside to dry.

★ Once they are dry, encourage the children to cut a cloud shape out of their bubble-painted papers.

★ Give each child a piece of black construction paper. Help the child cut out four rectangles for legs, a circle for a head, and two small circles for ears.

★ Encourage the children to glue the legs to the bottom of the cloud shape, the ears to the larger head circle, and the head circle to the cloud as the lamb's face. Help them glue two wiggle eyes to the head circle.

Supplies
clear liquid soap, water, black tempera paint, straws, white paper, scissors, black construction paper, glue, wiggle eyes

Find Bethlehem

Supplies
angel costume

Invite an adult or teenager to dress as and play the Angel for the following activity.

The Angel interrupts the arrival activities by saying:

Angel: "Don't be afraid! Look! I bring good news to you—wonderful, joyous news for all people. Your savior is born today in David's city. He is Christ the Lord. This is a sign for you: you will find a newborn baby wrapped snugly and lying in a manger" (Luke 2:10-12).

Hark! The Herald Angels Sing

Supplies
Reproducible 3a, pens or pencils, markers or crayons

An Angelic Message

Before Class: Photocopy "Angelic Message" **(Reproducible 3a)** for each child.

Say: The shepherds were in their fields one night when all of a sudden an angel appeared with a message. Use the decoder to find out what they said!

★ Hand out "Angelic Message" and a pen or pencil to each child.

★ Help the children use the decoder to fill in the blanks.

★ Encourage them to color the page once they are finished decoding the message.

Supplies
Reproducible 3d

Bible Story

Before Class: Photocopy "One Dark Night" **(Reproducible 3d)** for each child.

★ Assign the parts to the children so they can act out the story.

★ Act out the story.

Supplies
Reproducible 3b, glitter, glue, markers or crayons

Shepherds on the Hillside

Before Class: Photocopy "Shepherds on the Hillside" **(Reproducible 3b)** for each child.

★ Give each child "Shepherds on the Hillside" and markers or crayons to color the page.

★ Invite the children to draw the angels that visited the shepherds the night Jesus was born.

★ Encourage them to color the whole sheet.

★ Let them add glitter to the angels by putting glue on the page and sprinkling a bit of glitter over the glue.

Easy Coffee Filter Angel

★ Give each child three coffee filters, two cotton balls, one 6-inch to 8-inch piece of silver or gold ribbon, one white chenille stem, and one gold chenille stem.

★ Help the children place two cotton balls in the center of one of the coffee filters.

★ Encourage them to pinch the coffee filter with their fingers, gathering the cotton balls in the center to create the angel's head.

★ Help them place a second coffee filter onto the open end, tucking the filter in a bit into the head area. This will produce a layered effect for the dress.

★ While the children are still holding the filters together, help them tie a piece of gold or silver ribbon around the "neck" and tie a tight bow.

★ Show the children how to take the third coffee filter and fold it in half, then fold the filter up lengthwise accordion-style.

★ Help them wrap a white chenille stem around the center, and then fan out the wings. Show them how to fold the excess chenille into a loop for a hanger and twist the ends together.

★ Show the children how to make a halo from the gold chenille stem. Trim the hanging end of the chenille stem, leaving three inches.

★ After the children have assembled all of the pieces for their angels, hot glue the halo to the back of the angel so that it is positioned above the head, and glue the wings in place behind the angel, hiding the gold chenille of the halo connector. Only you or another adult should handle the glue gun.

Say: The Bible doesn't say exactly how the angels looked when they appeared to the shepherds, but that is not what's important. What we must remember when we read the story of Jesus' birth is that God sent Jesus to teach us about God's love. Shepherds were looked down on, but because the angelic messengers appeared to the shepherds first, we know that God loves all of us.

Make Angel Wings

★ Show each child how to draw an eye shape in the middle of eight paper plates. (This will give you two crescent shapes around the rim of the plates.)

★ Encourage the children to cut the eye shape out of each plate.

★ Recycle the eye shapes, leaving the crescents for the wing feathers.

Supplies
coffee filters, cotton balls, silver or gold ribbons in 6- to 8-inch pieces, white chenille stems, gold chenille stems, scissors, hot glue gun (adult use only)

Supplies
ten plain white paper plates per child, two 12-inch pieces of ribbon per child, pencils, glue, scissors

- ★ Help the child glue eight crescents to each side of a whole plate to make it look like wings.
- ★ Invite them to glue another whole plate onto the first plate (with feather-ends in between) to reinforce the feathers.
- ★ Encourage the children to flip the wings over. Help them glue two pieces of ribbon onto the plate as shoulder straps so they can wear the wings.

Bible Verse

Supplies
Bible, Reproducible 3c, scissors

Before Class: Photocopy and cut apart two sets of "Bible Verse Memory Cards" **(Reproducible 3c)**.

- ★ Invite the children to sit in a circle.
- ★ Hold open the Bible and read this session's Bible verse to the children: "Your savior is born today in David's city. He is Christ the Lord" (Luke 2:11).

Say: Let's practice our verse. Repeat after me: Your savior *(pause)* is born today *(pause)* in David's city *(pause)*. He is Christ *(pause)* the Lord *(pause)*.

- ★ Invite the children to join you in a game of memory.
- ★ Place the cards face-down on the table.
- ★ The children will take turns turning over two cards at a time. If the cards match the child may keep the set. If they do not, the child must put the cards back in their places face-down. Keep playing until all of the cards have been paired.
- ★ At the end of the game ask the children to arrange the cards in order of the Bible verse.

Teaching Tip
If you have a large group, prepare a second pair of card sets and have two games played separately.

Easy Handprint Angel

Supplies
skin-colored construction paper, blue construction paper, white paint, paper plate, smocks, gold chenille stems, scissors, black markers, hand-cleaning supplies, glue

Before Class: Cut out 2-inch circles from skin-colored construction paper for the faces of the angels. Cut gold chenille stems to fit the angels' heads as haloes.

- ★ Give each child a smock, a piece of blue construction paper, a face circle, a halo, and scissors.
- ★ Pour white paint onto a paper plate. One at a time, invite the children to place a hand in the white paint and then stamp it onto the blue construction paper with all fingers together.
- ★ Once their hands are clean, encourage the children to use markers to draw faces on their skin-colored circles.
- ★ Have them glue their angel's faces onto the palm side of their handprints. Their thumbs are the wings and their fingers are the robes. (The angel's body is seen from the side.)
- ★ Invite the children to glue the gold chenille stem to the angel's head as a halo.

Stop at the Guestroom

Divide the children into small groups. You may organize the groups around age levels or separate them into readers and nonreaders. Keep the groups small, with a maximum number of ten children in each group. You may need to have more than one group of each type. Make sure you have enough volunteers to manage each group.

Young Children

Say: Our adventures have taken us to a nearby shepherds' field. They were tending their flock when something happened.

Ask: What happened to the shepherds? *(An angel appeared.)*

Say: An angel of God appeared! The angel had a very special announcement that needed to be shared.

Ask: What was the announcement? *(Jesus was born.)*

Say: The message was a message of joy! Jesus, Christ the Lord, was born in Bethlehem that night.

Ask: If you had been a shepherd in the field that night, what would you have done when you saw the angels? *(Let the children respond.)* Would you have believed the angel's message? *(Let the children respond.)* What do you think the shepherds will do now that the angels have told them Jesus has been born? *(Let the children respond.)*

Say: In our next lesson we'll see what the shepherds decide to do with the special birth announcement the angels told to them. But right now we're going to make special lambs to help us remember the story of the shepherds. They were not rich or royal. They were hard workers who were outsiders of their community. God sent the angels to them to say to the world, "My love is for everyone. My son will teach all of you about my love." That's a message of great joy!

Make a Lamb

★ Pour white paint onto one paper plate and black paint onto a second paper plate.

★ Show the children how to dip their fingers in the white paint and make a large oval out of fingerprints on a piece of paper.

★ Have each child use black paint to add a thumbprint for the head and small fingerprints as the ears.

★ Have the child make four black fingerprints for the legs.

Say: Our Bible verse says, "Your savior is born today in David's city. He is Christ the Lord" (Luke 2:11). Let's remember the shepherds and the angels and the message that Jesus is here!

Supplies
white paint, black paint, paper plates, colored paper, hand-cleaning supplies

Older Children

Say: Our adventures have taken us to a shepherds' field near Bethlehem. Imagine that you are one of the shepherds on the hillside with your sheep: it's night, it's dark, and suddenly an angel appears bright in the sky, followed by a whole bunch of angels, and they are telling about the birth of the Savior.

Ask: How would you feel? *(Let the children respond.)* What questions would you have for the angels? *(Let the children respond.)* What would you have done? *(Let the children respond.)*

Say: Shepherds were not well regarded in biblical times. People thought that they were dirty and unclean because they worked in the fields with animals. Shepherds were also considered untrustworthy because people thought the shepherds would try to steal sheep.

Ask: Why do you think that the first people to hear about the birth of Jesus were shepherds? *(Let the children respond.)* Which groups today are like the shepherds who might be the first to hear about Jesus' birth if Jesus were born today? *(Let the children respond.)* Why? *(Let the children respond.)*

Say: In our next lesson we will see what the shepherds decide to do with the special birth announcement the angels told to them. Let's make special lambs to help us remember the story of the shepherds.

Make a Lamb

Supplies
white yarn, rectangles of stiff cardboard, rubber bands, scissors, black felt, glue, small gold bells, black chenille stems

★ Show each child how to make a lamb's body by loosely wrapping yarn around the width of a small cardboard rectangle until it has been covered at least three times. (The more yarn used, the fluffier the sheep's coat will be.)

★ When finished, help the child slide the yarn off of the cardboard onto her or his fingers, gathering all the loops together. Help the child use the other hand to put a rubber band tightly around the loops, cinching it in the center like an hourglass.

★ Help the child cut through the loops on both ends of the hourglass and fluff up the pom-pom. If the yarn pieces are uneven, have the child "shear" the sheep with the scissors.

★ Let the child cut a face shape out of felt. Then have the child glue it and a bell onto one end of the sheep.

★ Have the child cut a black chenille stem in half and bend each half into a U shape. Show the child how to thread the two pieces through the center of the sheep's body, so that they stick down on each side like legs.

Say: Our Bible verse says, "Your savior is born today in David's city. He is Christ the Lord" (Luke 2:11). Let's remember the shepherds, the angels, and the message that Jesus is here!

Angelic Message

| A | I | O | R | S | U | V | Y |

born today in David's city. He is Christ the Lord.

—Luke 2:11

Shepherds on the Hillside

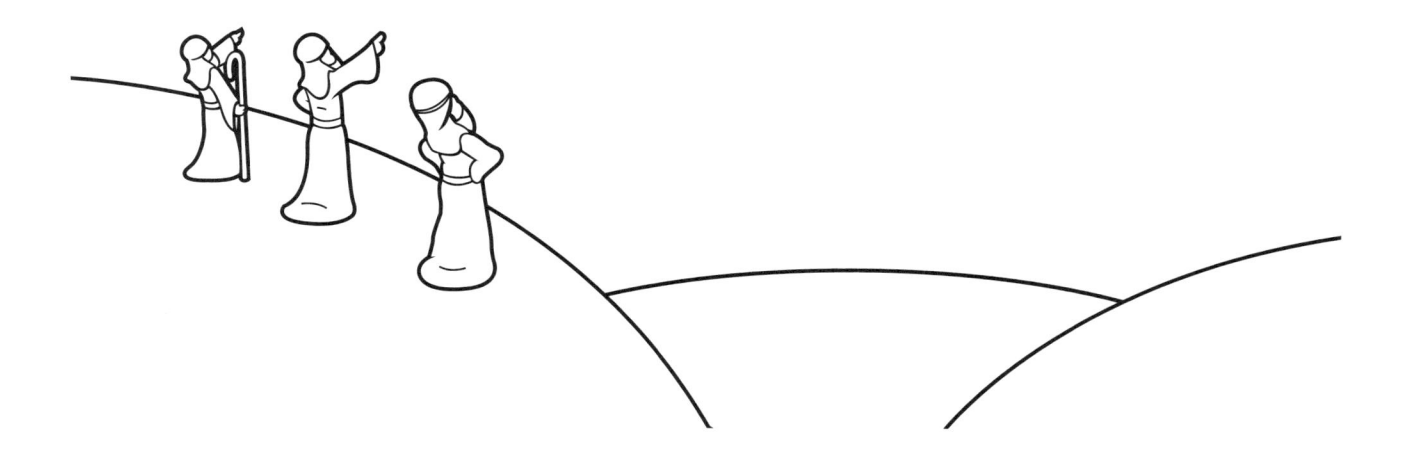

3c # Bible Verse Memory Cards

Your	savior	is
born	today	in
David's	city.	He is
Christ	the	Lord.

One Dark Night

by LeeDell Stickler

Characters: *Bible Storyteller, Shepherd 1, Shepherd 2, Shepherd 3, Angel, Extra Shepherds, Extra Angels*

Bible Storyteller: Long ago in the hills outside of Bethlehem, a group of shepherds drew close around the fire.

Shepherd 1: Put more sticks on the fire. I'm cold and it's dark.

Shepherd 2: You're always cold! But it isn't so dark at all.

Shepherd 3: That's not the fire. That light is coming from the sky. Look! *(points to the sky)*

Shepherd 1: It's getting brighter and brighter. What is it? I've never seen anything like this before.

Shepherd 2: Neither have I! The sky is on fire. The world must be coming to an end!

All Shepherds: Help! Help!

Shepherd 3: Wait. Look. In the light. Is that a person? Could it be an angel?

Shepherd 1: I don't know what an angel looks like.

Shepherd 2: What would an angel want with us? We're shepherds, for goodness' sakes.

Shepherd 3: Well, I think it's an angel. And I'm scared!

Angel: Don't be afraid! I have come to bring you good news!

All Shepherds: Good news?

Angel: Good news that will bring great joy to all people! Your Savior has been born this very night!

Shepherd 1: The Savior? The one we have been waiting for?

Shepherd 2: Where can we find him?

Angel: You will find him in Bethlehem, lying in a manger.

Bible Storyteller: Suddenly the sky grew even brighter than before as more angels appeared. Then the angels began to sing.

Angels: Glory to God in the highest and peace to people of earth!

Shepherd 3: Where did they go? They just disappeared!

Shepherd 1: We need to find this child that the angel told us about.

Shepherd 2: Let's go right now into Bethlehem!

Permission is granted to duplicate this page for local church use only. © 2013 Abingdon Press.

4 The Shepherds' Adventure

Objectives
The children will:
★ hear Luke 2:15-20;
★ share in the shepherds' praise;
★ continue the journey to discover Christ's light on Christmas.

Bible Story
Luke 2:15-20

Bible Verse
When they saw this, they reported what they had been told about this child. Everyone who heard it was amazed at what the shepherds told them. (Luke 2:17-18)

Focus for the Teacher

The Bible Verse
We have traveled from Nazareth to Bethlehem with Mary and Joseph, and we have met the shepherds and the angels who announced the Savior's birth. We know the shepherds will respond to this angelic message by rushing off to find the baby Messiah. Today we'll go with the shepherds from the fields to the manger and then out into the streets of Bethlehem as they share the message of the newborn Savior.

Shepherds
The reaction of the shepherds has always been an exemplary instance of faith. The angels interrupt the shepherds' evening by sharing with them a message of the newborn Messiah, and the shepherds, without hesitation, jump to the occasion to go find him. They find the baby lying in a manger and tell Mary about the message the angels gave to them. The next part is important: then the shepherds go and tell this message to others. They tell people about their experience with the angels and about the baby lying in the manger. They did not keep their findings to themselves. They found the Savior and shared the Savior with everyone who would listen.

In our world today not many people would make the same choices that the shepherds did. They might try to explain the multitude of angels as some scientific phenomenon or ignore the message because they had work to do. Even if we believe what we have heard and go to find the Messiah, we may not have the willingness, or bravery, to share what we have experienced. Our children need to be reminded, and shown, that faith is something to claim and share.

Finding Bethlehem
"We need a Savior! We have a Savior! And, we can share the Savior!"
—James Moore

This lesson is so important for us all. The shepherds' faith reminds us that we need a Savior, we have a Savior, and we can share the Savior with others.

Begin the Journey

Be sure that adult leaders are waiting when the first child arrives. Greet and welcome each child. Get the child involved in an activity that interests him or her and introduces the theme for the session.

Say: We began our adventure by traveling with Mary and Joseph from Nazareth to Bethlehem. They had to travel the ninety miles, which took ten days, to be counted. When they got to a very busy Bethlehem they could not find a place to stay and ended up staying in a stable. Jesus was born that night in that stable. Mary wrapped him in cloths and laid him in a manger.

Say: Our adventure then led us to a nearby shepherds' field, where a multitude of heavenly hosts announced the birth of Jesus to a group of shepherds. This time we will find out what the shepherds did with the message the angels gave to them.

The Shepherds Find the Baby

Following the Shepherds

- ★ Invite the children to form a circle.
- ★ Choose one child to be the guesser. Remove the guesser from the circle and place her or him in a part of the room where this child can't see or hear anything.
- ★ Choose a leader from the remaining children. Tell the children that they need to follow the movements of the leader without making it obvious which child is the leader.
- ★ Invite the guesser back to the group and have her or him stand in the center of the circle.
- ★ All the children should begin swinging their arms back and forth. The leader should eventually start to make additional movements that the rest begin to mimic.
- ★ The child in the center gets three guesses to find the leader. Then choose a new guesser and leader. Play several times so everyone has an opportunity to be the leader and the guesser.

Say: Now we will follow the shepherds from the field into the town of Bethlehem to find the baby Messiah, Jesus.

Shepherd's Crook Snack

Before Class: Preheat the oven following the instructions on the can of dough. Place a sheet of wax paper on the baking sheet.

- ★ Have the children wash their hands.
- ★ Hand out a paper plate with a piece of breadstick dough to each child.

Supplies
refrigerated breadstick dough, paper plates, wax paper, baking sheet

- ★ Show the children how to bend a breadstick into a shepherd's crook.
- ★ Let the children place their breadsticks onto the baking sheet.
- ★ Bake the breadsticks according to the can's instructions. When they are finished baking, set them aside for Stop at the Guestroom.

Say: Shepherds used crooks to pull the sheep back in if they strayed away from the group. The shepherds would hold on to the bottom part of the crook and put the "crooked" part around the neck of a sheep to pull it to safety.

The Shepherds Look for Jesus

Before Class: Photocopy the "Shepherds Maze" (**Reproducible 4a**) for each child.

Say: The shepherds left the field and went to Bethlehem in search of baby Jesus. Once they found Jesus, they went through Bethlehem to tell everyone about their adventure. Let's help the shepherds in our maze find Jesus and tell others.

- ★ Give each child "Shepherds Maze" and crayons or markers.
- ★ Encourage them to complete the maze.
- ★ Invite each child to color the picture.

The Shepherds Praised God

Before Class: Cut egg cartons into separate cups and cut string into 3-inch pieces. Use the point of the scissors or a sharp pencil to poke a hole in the bottom of each egg cup.

Say: The shepherds saw baby Jesus and praised God for sending the Savior. We can praise God for our blessings, too. One way we can praise God is by making happy music. We're going to make bells so we can make happy music for God.

- ★ Give each child an egg cup.
- ★ Invite the children to decorate their cups however they like with paints. You can mix glitter into the paints for a quick colorful sparkle effect.
- ★ Give each child a piece of string and help the child tie a small bell onto one end.
- ★ Show the children how to thread the string through the hole in the egg cup. Pull the string all the way through until the bell hits the inside of the cup.
- ★ Help each child tie a knot at the top of the egg cup to hold the bell securely in place.
- ★ Demonstrate how to form a loop with the remaining string.

Teaching Tip
Allow the children to participate in the other lesson activities while the crooks bake.

Always check for allergies before preparing or serving food.

Supplies
Reproducible 4a, crayons or markers

Supplies
egg cartons, scissors, string, jingle bells or other small bells, glitter, paint, paintbrushes, smocks

Teaching Tip
For easier cleanup, use markers instead of paint.

Find Bethlehem

Supplies
Bible-times costume

Invite an adult or teenager to dress as and play the shepherd for the following activity.

The Shepherd interrupts the activities by saying:

Shepherd: You will not believe what just happened! I was with the other shepherds and we were lying out in the field with the sheep. It was getting kind of cold, but I was starting to sleep. Guess what happened! An angel of the Lord appeared! The angel told us that the Savior had been born in a stable in Bethlehem. We would find the baby wrapped in cloths and lying in a feeding trough. So, we all got up and ran into town. We wandered around until we found the baby and his parents, Mary and Joseph. It is the Savior, I tell you!

The Shepherds Share the Good News

Tweet the Good News

Supplies
Reproducible 4b, pens or pencils, crayons or markers

Before Class: Photocopy "Tweet the Good News" **(Reproducible 4b)** for each child.

Say: The shepherds were so happy they had found Jesus that they wanted to tell everyone.

Ask: Today, how would you tell everyone you know about good news?

Say: We're going to "Tweet the Good News" by writing a sentence about your favorite part of the Christmas story.

★ Hand out "Tweet the Good News" and a pen or pencil to each child.

★ Encourage the children to write their favorite part of the Christmas story. If you have a child who does not write, invite the child to draw her or his favorite part.

★ Encourage the children to color the pages once they are finished and then display their tweets around the church for everyone to see.

Bible Story

Supplies
Reproducible 4d, costumes for the shepherds and townspeople

Before Class: Photocopy "Shepherds Announce the Savior's Birth" **(Reproducible 4d)** for each actor. Arrange for adults or youth to act out the story.

★ Invite the children to sit and watch while the actors perform the drama.

Shepherds Tag

Say: The shepherds shared the good news with everyone who would listen.

Ask: Do you think the people the shepherds told about Jesus told other people about Jesus, too?

Say: I bet they did! In our game we will be sharing the good news by tagging each other. Once you have been tagged, you should share the good news with, or tag, your classmates.

★ Choose a child to be the shepherd.

★ The shepherd will tag the other children.

★ Each child who is tagged becomes a shepherd too.

★ The shepherds will continue to tag until every child has been tagged.

★ Play this game a few times so everyone has a turn being the first shepherd.

Praising Shepherds

Before Class: Photocopy "Praise God" **(Reproducible 4c, top)** for each child. Cut off the announcement strip and save it for later.

Say: The shepherds were so excited to meet baby Jesus, the Savior, that they praised God. We can praise God by singing.

While shepherds kept their watching
Over silent flocks by night,
Behold throughout the heavens
There shone a holy light:
Go, tell it on the mountain,
Over the hills and everywhere;
Go, tell it on the mountain
That Jesus Christ is born.

The shepherds feared and trembled
When lo! above the earth
Rang out the angel chorus
That hailed the Savior's birth:
Go, tell it on the mountain,
Over the hills and everywhere;
Go, tell it on the mountain
That Jesus Christ is born.

Say: Let's write our own praise song to share the good news about Jesus.

★ Hand out "Praise God." Encourage the children to fill in the blanks of the song.

　★ When everyone is finished, invite the children to share their praises with the class.

Good News Echo

★ Invite the children to repeat each line after you and do the motion you show them. Point to the children when it is their turn—you may have to echo the line with them.

Supplies
Reproducible 4c, scissors, pens or pencils

(Put hand to ear as if to hear better.)

Teacher: Have you heard, have you heard, have you heard the news today?

Echo: Have you heard, have you heard, have you heard the news today?

(Put fingers of both hands together above head to form a roof.)

Teacher: In a barn, in a barn, in a manger full of hay.

Echo: In a barn, in a barn, in a manger full of hay.

(Flap wings for rooster, use hands as ears for donkeys, use fingers like horns for cattle, wave hands joyfully over head for shepherds.)

Teacher: The roosters crow, the donkeys bray, the cattle moo, and the shepherds say—

Echo: The roosters crow, the donkeys bray, the cattle moo, and the shepherds say—

(Continue to wave hands joyfully above head.)

Teacher: Hallelujah, hallelujah, Jesus Christ is born today!

Echo: Hallelujah, hallelujah, Jesus Christ is born today!

Say: The shepherds were so full of joy that they praised God and told everyone that Jesus was born. We can share the good news too!

Bible Verse

Before Class: Write the memory verse on the chalkboard.

★ Invite the children to sit in a circle.

★ Hold open the Bible and read this session's Bible verse to the children: "When they saw this, they reported what they had been told about this child. Everyone who heard it was amazed at what the shepherds told them" (Luke 2:17-18).

Say: Let's practice our verse. Repeat after me: When they saw this *(pause)*, they reported what they *(pause)* had been told *(pause)* about this child *(pause)*. Everyone who heard it *(pause)* was amazed at what *(pause)* the shepherds told them *(pause)*.

★ After you practice the verse a couple of times with the class, cover one of the words on the board by taping an index card over it.

★ Encourage the children to fill in the blank as they recite the verse again.

★ Continue until all of the words have been covered and the children can recite the verse on their own.

Supplies
Bible; chalkboard and chalk, or bulletin board paper and marker; index cards; tape

Stop at the Guestroom

Divide the children into small groups. You may organize the groups around age levels or separate them into readers and nonreaders. Keep the groups small, with a maximum number of ten children in each group. You may need to have more than one group of each type. Make sure you have enough volunteers to manage each group.

Young Children

Say: After the shepherds saw Jesus they told Mary about the angels. Then they ran into Bethlehem and told everyone about Jesus. They praised God for the blessings of the Savior.

Ask: How do you praise God for your blessings? *(Let the children respond.)* Do you tell others about God's blessings?

Say: In our next lesson we'll return from our journeys. Now that we have found baby Jesus in Bethlehem, what should we do? We'll find out next time what God asks all of us to do.

Say: Right now let's make a birth announcement. When a new baby is born, birth announcements are sent out to let others know of the good news. Today we've experienced the shepherds announcing Jesus' birth. We can remember what they did when we see our birth announcements for Jesus.

Make a Birth Announcement

Before Class: Photocopy and cut out "Announcement" **(Reproducible 4c, bottom)** for each child. Cut construction paper in half, cut skin-colored paper into 1-inch circles and white paper into 2-inch by 1-inch rectangles.

★ Give each child the announcement strip and half a piece of construction paper. Help each child turn the paper so it looks like a postcard. Help each child glue the announcement caption at the top of the construction paper.

★ Show each child how to glue two craft sticks in a wide X in the center of their papers. Encourage the children to glue shredded paper on top of the X to look like hay.

★ Have each child glue a circle (Jesus' face) and a rectangle (Jesus' blanket) onto the hay. Encourage the child to add eyes and a smile to Jesus' face using a marker.

Share the Shepherd's Crook Snacks

★ Have the children wash their hands.
★ Hand out a plate, a cup of water, and a shepherd's crook snack to each child.

Supplies
Reproducible 4c (bottom), scissors, construction paper, skin-colored paper, white paper, markers, craft sticks, shredded paper, glue

Teaching Tip
Check for allergies before serving food.

Supplies
plates, cups, water, shepherd's crook snacks

Older Children

Say: Today our adventures have taken us from a shepherds' field to a baby in a manger and out into the streets of Bethlehem. We praised God for baby Jesus, and we shared that good news with our classmates. Jesus, our Savior, has been born! What joyous news this is!

Ask: What did the shepherds do after the angels announced the birth of Jesus? *(Let the children respond.)* What would you have done if the angels had come to you with this announcement? *(Let the children respond.)*

Say: The shepherds ran to find Jesus. Once they had found him, they told Mary about the angels. Then they ran into Bethlehem and told everyone about baby Jesus and praised God for the blessings of the baby Savior.

Ask: How do you praise God for your blessings? Do you tell others about God's blessings?

Say: In our next lesson we will return from our journeys. Now that we have found baby Jesus in Bethlehem, what should we do? We'll find out next time what God asks all of us to do.

Say: Right now we are going to make a birth announcement. When a new baby is born, birth announcements are sent out to let others know of the good news. Today we have experienced the shepherds announcing Jesus' birth. We can remember what they did when we see our birth announcements for Jesus.

Make a Birth Announcement

★ Give each child a piece of construction paper, a marker, and a Bible.

★ Encourage the children to use their Bibles to write a birth announcement for Jesus. Invite them to find the details of where, when, and to whom Jesus was born. They can include all of these details in their announcement.

★ Have them draw a picture of the Nativity scene on the announcement.

Share the Shepherd's Crook Snacks

★ Encourage the children to wash their hands.

★ Hand out a plate, a cup of water, and a shepherd's crook snack to each child.

Supplies
Bibles, construction paper, markers

Supplies
plates, cups, water, shepherd's crook snacks made earlier

Teaching Tip
Check for allergies before serving food.

4a Shepherds Maze

Help the shepherds find the baby Jesus. Then help them find their way home and share the good news along the way.

START

END

Permission is granted to duplicate this page for local church use only. © 2013 Abingdon Press.

Tweet the Good News

4c Praise God / Announcement

Make choices from the word box below to complete this praise song.

God you are so _____!

You have done many great things for me. I am so _____ for/by them all.

A few blessings you have given me are:

_____   _____   _____

Pick one of these words to go in the first blank:
    strong   loving   graceful   kind   gentle

Pick one of these words to go in the second blank:
    thankful   happy   satisfied   grateful   pleased

Pick any three of these phrases to go in the last three blanks:

a great family	good friends	a church
food to eat	a warm bed	a loving teacher
a dog	a cat	people who care about me
		a house to live in

Announcing the Birth of Jesus

Permission is granted to duplicate this page for local church use only. © 2013 Abingdon Press.

Shepherds Announce the Savior's Birth
by LeeDell Stickler

Characters: *Shepherd 1, Shepherd 2, Shepherd 3, Townsperson 1, Townsperson 2, Townsperson 3*

Shepherd 1: *(to townsperson)* Did you hear the news? The Messiah has been born—right here in Bethlehem!

Townsperson 1: The Savior? Here in Bethlehem? How do you know?

Shepherd 2: The angels told us.

Townsperson 2: Angels? What would angels want with the likes of you?

Shepherd 3: We wondered that ourselves. We couldn't come up with an answer. But there we were . . .

Shepherd 1: Out on the hillside . . .

Shepherd 2: Keeping watch over our flocks.

Shepherd 3: And it was nighttime.

Shepherd 1: Suddenly they were there.

Shepherd 2: Hundreds and hundreds of angels.

Shepherd 3: The sky was filled with angels.

Shepherd 1: And they told us about the Messiah.

Townsperson 3: Did they tell you where to find the Messiah? I'm certain there were several babies born this very night.

Shepherd 2: They did. They said the Messiah would be wrapped in bands of cloth and lying in a manger.

Townsperson 1: Hmmm. This is unusual. Not many babies sleep in a feed trough.

Townsperson 2: That's for sure.

Townsperson 3: Is that all? Did you check it out for yourselves?

Shepherd 3: We did. We had to see. And he was there . . .

Shepherd 1: Just as the angels had said . . .

Shepherd 2: In a manger in a stable . . .

Shepherd 3: And we saw his mother, Mary. We told her about the angels.

Shepherd 1: And now we are telling you.

Shepherds: The Messiah is born! Glory to God in the highest heaven, and on earth peace among those whom God favors!

Permission is granted to duplicate this page for local church use only. © 2013 Abingdon Press.

5. Share Our Findings

Objectives

The children will:
- hear Luke 2:1-20;
- review our adventures;
- share the love and light of Christ.

Bible Story

Luke 2:1-20

Bible Verse

The light shines in the darkness, and the darkness doesn't extinguish the light. (John 1:5)

Focus for the Teacher

The Bible Story

Your class has now experienced Luke's narrative of Jesus' birth story. Mary and Joseph have traveled to Bethlehem as a family merely participating in life. The shepherds have gone to Bethlehem because of a divine, miraculous experience. This gives us two examples of encountering God, in the midst of the ordinary and in the midst of miracles. We are all called to Bethlehem. Bethlehem represents the hope, love, joy, and peace that God sends to us in the form of a baby. Jesus comes as a light in the darkness of our world. Bethlehem breaks into the bedlam.

The Bible Verse

The Book of John is very metaphorical and quite different from the other Gospel books. In the opening of John we see an attempt at describing the magnificence of the Word, Jesus. The verse we will focus on in this session compares Jesus to the light. The ability to give and sustain life is symbolized by the light, which is an appropriate metaphor for Jesus. The resilience of the light that shines in the darkness is confirmation of the power of life available in the Word.

Finding Bethlehem

"When the writers of the Bible tried to express the inexpressible, they used analogies, stories, or comparisons to make their points. When the truth that they wanted to express was too big for words, they searched for dramatic illustrations that could somehow convey the heart of their message. That's what we find in our Scripture lesson for this chapter. How do you express the birth of Jesus Christ to our world? How do you do justice to his birth? How do you capture its impact? How do you communicate what it means? Words were inadequate, so they tried to express it through dramatic poetic analogy. They compared it to light coming into the world of darkness! Now, that's a dramatic way to put it, isn't it? It was dark, and then light came. It was dark, and the light turned on. God's light came into our dark world."—James Moore

Continue the Journey

Be sure that adult leaders are waiting when the first child arrives. Greet and welcome each child. Get the child involved in an activity that interests him or her and introduces the theme for the session.

Say: Our adventure has led us to Bethlehem alongside Mary and Joseph, as well as alongside the shepherds. Mary and Joseph set out to find Bethlehem because of a Roman decree. They were following the rules of their everyday lives. The shepherds went to Bethlehem because of a heavenly encounter with God's angels. We are all invited to find Bethlehem. Sometimes we get there through the day-to-day things, and sometimes we get there through miracles.

Say: We have gone to Bethlehem and returned. We saw God's greatest gift, Jesus! He grows up and teaches us all about the love God has for each of us. Our Bibles call Jesus the Light of the World.

Ask: What do you think that means?

Say: The Bible calls Jesus the Light of the World because even in our hardest times, Jesus is still there. Jesus never goes away, just like the light never goes away no matter how dark it gets. We found the Light of the World in Bethlehem.

Ask: Now that we have found Bethlehem, what should we do?

Experience the Light

Drama Center

Supplies
baby doll; dress-up clothes for Mary, Joseph, the shepherds, and the angels; stuffed animal lambs

★ Encourage the children to dress up like Mary, Joseph, the shepherds, or the angels.

★ Invite them to act out the Nativity story they have been learning.

Say: Mary and Joseph went to Bethlehem for the census. While there, they had baby Jesus. God's angels appeared to the shepherds and told the shepherds about the special baby Jesus in Bethlehem. The shepherds then ran to Bethlehem to find the baby. We celebrate the birth of Jesus at Christmas.

Christmas Candle

Supplies
Reproducible 5a, glow-in-the-dark crayons or paints, cardstock if using paints

Before Class: Photocopy "Christmas Candle" **(Reproducible 5a)** for each child. Use cardstock paper if the children will be painting it.

★ Give each child "Christmas Candle" and something to color the picture with.

Say: Candles are used at church to help us remember Jesus, the Light of the World. We see them on the altar at a lot of churches. We also use candles during Advent, the time leading up to Christmas. Advent candles help us remember the hope, love, joy, and peace Jesus gives us.

Light Exploration Center

Before Class: Locate or construct a light box (see below). Collect various objects that allow light to pass through them, such as marbles, prisms, picture slides, and translucent jewels or beads. Make a tent using a large blanket and chairs.

★ Set out on the light box the objects you gathered.

★ Invite the children to explore light using the light box and explore darkness by playing in the tent.

Ask: What does light do? What is darkness like? Can you see in the dark? What helps you see? Is it completely dark in the tent?

Say: There is always light. Our Bible calls Jesus the Light of the World.

Ask: Do you think Jesus is like a light in the darkness? Why?

Supplies
a light box, objects light can pass through, large blanket, chairs

Teaching Tip
The more children understand how light works, the easier it will be to translate for them the abstract metaphor about Jesus being the Light of the World.

Make Your Own Light Box

★ Line the inside of the lid of a storage tub with sheets of tracing paper. This will dull the light and help it to be dispersed more evenly. Secure the paper with tape.

★ Put the Christmas lights into the box and spread them out. Let the end of the lights come out at one corner so they can be plugged in. The lid will still fit over the top.

★ Put the lid on, and turn on the lights in the box.

Supplies
a large translucent storage tub, large sheets of tracing paper, tape, 2 strings of Christmas lights

Flashlight Tag

★ Find an open, barely lit space. It also helps if there are a few places to hide.

★ Choose one child to be IT. IT will use the flashlight to "tag" people.

★ Encourage IT to count to thirty while the class hides.

★ IT will then go look for people. To tag someone, IT must shine a light on the person and say that person's name.

★ Play until everyone is tagged. The first one caught will be IT in the next round.

★ Play a few rounds until everyone who wants to be IT gets a turn.

Say: The light in our game helped us see each other. We need light in the darkness, just like we need Jesus.

Supplies
a flashlight, a barely lit open area

Teaching Tip
Caution the children to avoid shining the flashlight directly into people's eyes.

Share the Light

Invite the children to join you for the following activities.

Candle Marshmallow Pops

Supplies
five marshmallows per child, toothpicks, water, bowls, yellow colored sugar, purple colored sugar, lollipop sticks, clean kitchen scissors, wax paper, paper towels

Before Class: Prepare a workstation where the children will come to you for help with this project. This should have a bowl of water, a paper towel, toothpicks, an empty bowl or plate, colored sugar, lollipop sticks, and a piece of wax paper.

★ Give each child a small piece of wax paper and five marshmallows.

★ Help each child cut one of the marshmallows to look like a flame.

★ Invite children to your station a few at a time.

★ Using a toothpick to hold one marshmallow, encourage the child to submerge the marshmallow fully in the water and remove it quickly. Help dab the excess water on the paper towel.

★ Invite the child to hold the marshmallow over the empty bowl and sprinkle generously with colored sugar to entirely coat the marshmallow. Use yellow sugar for the flame and purple for the other four marshmallows.

★ Help the children carefully remove each marshmallow from the toothpick and set it on a piece of wax paper to dry.

★ Once all five marshmallows have been prepared, give the child one lollipop stick. The child should use the holes left by the toothpicks to push marshmallows down over the stick one by one: four purple ones and then a yellow flame on top.

★ Set the candle marshmallow pops aside for Guestroom time.

Say: Advent, the time we prepare for Jesus' birth, uses candles to help us get ready for Jesus. The purple candles look like our marshmallow pops. Advent candles help us remember the hope, love, joy, and peace Jesus gives us.

Teaching Tip
Check for allergies before preparing food.

Bible Story

Supplies
Reproducible 5d

Before Class: Photocopy "Praise God! Jesus Is Born!" **(Reproducible 5d)** for the reader.

★ Invite an adult or older child to read the story.

★ Have the children sit and participate in the story.

★ Assign parts for the children to help in the story. You might need to point to the child (or children) entrusted with each sound effect at the appropriate parts of the story.

You will need these parts:

- ★ **Trumpets:** Make a trumpet sound.
- ★ **Donkey hooves:** Pat right and left knees alternately.
- ★ **Crowd:** Repeat the phrase "peas and carrots" over and over again.
- ★ **Door:** Knock on a piece of wood, a wooden table, or a book.
- ★ **Animals in the stable:** Make a variety of animal sounds (cow, sheep, donkey, rooster, mouse, dove).
- ★ **Chorus:** Say "Praise God! Jesus is born!"

Salt Dough Candle Holders

Say: Let's make candle holders to give away to someone else. These candle holders will help us to share the good news that Jesus, the Light of the World, is born!

- ★ Encourage the children to help you make the salt dough.
    - Mix the dry ingredients in a bowl.
    - Add the oil.
    - Stir in the boiling water (only an adult should handle the boiling water) and allow it to cool briefly.
    - Knead the mixture into workable dough on a floured surface using your hands.
    - After a few minutes it should be soft and smooth and none should come off on your fingers. If it's still a little sticky then add more flour, one tablespoon at a time, until it's no longer sticky.
- ★ Give each child a fist-sized ball of salt dough on a paper plate.
- ★ Encourage the children to use their thumbs to press out a space in the center of the candle holder for a tea light candle.
- ★ Invite them to press sequins, glitter, or beads onto the candle holder to decorate it.
- ★ Leave the candle holders on the plates to dry.

Supplies
2 cups flour, 1 cup salt, 2 tablespoons oil, 2 tablespoons cream of tartar, 1.5 cups of boiling water; microwave to heat water, extra flour, large bowl, spoon, paper plates, tea light candles, sequins, glitter, beads

Sing-Along

Before Class: Photocopy "Sing-Along" **(Reproducible 5b)** for each child.

Say: Jesus is the Light of the World. Let's celebrate the hope, love, joy, and peace we receive from him on Christmas and all year long.

- ★ Invite your class to sing "L-I-G-H-T" and "This Little Light of Mine" along with you.

Supplies
Reproducible 5b

Suggested Messages
Jesus was born in a manger; There was no room in the guestroom; Jesus was born in Bethlehem; An angel visited the shepherds.

Supplies
Bible, Reproducible 5c, cardstock, crayons or markers, scissors

Supplies
wax paper, gold glitter glue, other colors of glitter glue, paper, markers, magnet stickers

Teaching Tip
If some of the glitter glue has not dried on the back, simply return it to the wax paper and wait longer.

Good News Telephone

Say: Jesus' birth is good news! The shepherds shared the good news of Jesus' birth with everyone they met. We can do the same.

★ Invite the children to sit in a circle.

★ Play the traditional telephone game, whispering messages about Jesus' birth around the circle.

Bible Verse

Before Class: Photocopy "Memory Verse Puzzle" **(Reproducible 5c)** on cardstock for each child.

★ Invite the children to sit in a circle.

★ Hold open the Bible and read this session's Bible verse to the children: "The light shines in the darkness, and the darkness doesn't extinguish the light" (John 1:5).

Say: Let's practice our verse. Repeat after me: The light shines (pause) in the darkness (pause), and the darkness doesn't (pause) extinguish the light (pause).

★ Practice the verse a couple of times with the class.

★ Hand out the "Memory Verse Puzzle" to each child. Encourage the children to color the picture and then to cut the pieces out.

★ Invite them to put the puzzles back together.

Glitter Glue Candles

★ Give each child a piece of wax paper and a piece of plain paper.

★ Invite the children to draw a simple candle with a flame on their pieces of regular paper.

★ Have the children set wax paper over their candle drawings.

★ Help them use glitter glue on top of the wax paper to trace and color in the drawing. Encourage them to use gold for the flame and another color for the candle. (Make sure the flame is fully connected to the candle.)

★ Set the glue candles aside to dry.

★ When they are dry, encourage the children to carefully remove their candles from the wax paper.

★ Let the children stick magnets on the back of their candles.

★ Encourage each child to find someone at church today to give the candle to as a way of sharing the light of Christ.

Stop at the Guestroom

Divide the children into small groups. You may organize the groups around age levels or separate them into readers and nonreaders. Keep the groups small, with a maximum number of ten children in each group. You may need to have more than one group of each type. Make sure you have enough volunteers to manage each group.

Young Children

Say: We have gone to Bethlehem and have returned. We saw God's greatest gift, Jesus! Jesus grows up and teaches us all about the love God has for each of us. Our Bibles call Jesus the Light of the World.

Ask: What do you think that means?

Say: The Bible calls Jesus the Light of the World because even in our hardest times, Jesus is still there. Jesus never goes away, just like the light never goes away no matter how dark it gets. We found the Light of the World in Bethlehem.

Ask: Now that we have found Bethlehem, what should we do?

Make a Paper Candle

Before Class: Cut out a 1-inch by 4-inch rectangle for each child from colored cardstock to serve as a candle.

- ★ Give each child a craft stick and a colored rectangle.
- ★ Encourage the children to glue the rectangle onto the craft stick, leaving room at the top of the craft stick for the tissue paper flame.
- ★ Invite the children to tear tissue paper into squares, and then glue the squares to the top of the craft sticks to look like flames.
- ★ Help the children write "Jesus" vertically down the front of their candles.
- ★ Invite them to glue magnets to the back of the craft sticks.
- ★ Encourage them to stick their Jesus candle on the refrigerator at home as a reminder to share the Light with others.

Share the Candle Marshmallow Pops

- ★ Have the children wash their hands.
- ★ Hand out a plate, a cup of water, and a candle marshmallow pop to each child.
- ★ Enjoy the snack while you review the lessons with the children.

Supplies
colored cardstock, scissors, large craft sticks, orange and yellow tissue paper, glue sticks, markers, magnet strips

Teaching Tip
Check for allergies before serving food.

Supplies
candle marshmallow snacks made earlier, plates, cups, water

Older Children

Say: We have gone to Bethlehem and have returned. We saw God's greatest gift, Jesus! Jesus grows up and teaches us all about the love God has for each of us. Our Bibles call Jesus the Light of the World.

Ask: What do you think that means?

Say: The Bible calls Jesus the Light of the World because even in our hardest times, Jesus is still there. Jesus never goes away, just like the light never goes away no matter how dark it gets. We found the Light of the World in Bethlehem.

Ask: Now that we have found Bethlehem, what should we do?

Make Quilling Paper Candles

Supplies
yellow paper, purple paper, construction paper, scissors, clear tape, glue

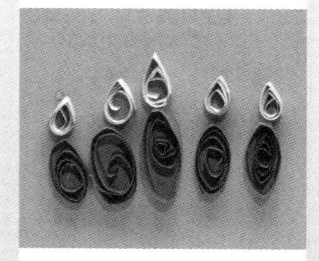

Before Class: Cut yellow and purple paper into strips ¼ inch wide. Cut construction paper in half.

★ Give each child five strips of yellow paper and five strips of purple paper. Each child will also need a half-sheet of construction paper and glue.

★ Demonstrate how to roll a yellow strip into a tight coil. (The coil should be level like a roll of tape on its side, not stretched in a spiral like a telephone cord.) Once it's rolled up, keep the coil level but shape it into a teardrop; pinch the tip to make the point stay. You may need to tape the loose ends closed. This will look like a flame. Do this with all five yellow strips.

★ Encourage the children to roll each purple strip into a coil, and then shape these coils into rectangles.

★ Invite the children to glue their rectangles and teardrops onto their construction paper to look like candles in a row.

★ Encourage them to take their candle pictures home and hang them somewhere to remind them to share the light with others.

Share the Candle Marshmallow Pops

Supplies
candle marshmallow snacks made earlier, plates, cups, water

Teaching Tip
Check for allergies before serving food.

★ Have the children wash their hands.

★ Hand out a plate, a cup of water, and a candle marshmallow pop to each child.

★ Enjoy the snack while you review the lessons with the children.

Christmas Candle

Sing-Along

L-I-G-H-T
Tune: Bingo

Oh, Jesus came to give us light,
And his light shines forever.
L-I-G-H-T,
L-I-G-H-T,
L-I-G-H-T,
And his light shines forever.

Oh, Jesus came to give us light,
And his light shines forever.
(clap)-I-G-H-T,
(clap)-I-G-H-T,
(clap)-I-G-H-T,
And his light shines forever.

Oh, Jesus came to give us light,
And his light shines forever.
(clap)-(clap)-G-H-T,
(clap)-(clap)-G-H-T,
(clap)-(clap)-G-H-T,
And his light shines forever.

Oh, Jesus came to give us light,
And his light shines forever.
(clap)-(clap)-(clap)-H-T,
(clap)-(clap)-(clap)-H-T,
(clap)-(clap)-(clap)-H-T,
And his light shines forever.

Oh, Jesus came to give us light,
And his light shines forever.
(clap)-(clap)-(clap)-(clap)-T,
(clap)-(clap)-(clap)-(clap)-T,
(clap)-(clap)-(clap)-(clap)-T,
And his light shines forever.

Oh, Jesus came to give us light,
And his light shines forever.
(clap)-(clap)-(clap)-(clap)-(clap),
(clap)-(clap)-(clap)-(clap)-(clap),
(clap)-(clap)-(clap)-(clap)-(clap),
And his light shines forever.

This Little Light of Mine
Words and music by Harry Dixon Loes

This little light of mine,
I'm gonna let it shine.
This little light of mine,
I'm gonna let it shine.
This little light of mine,
I'm gonna let it shine,
Let it shine, let it shine, let it shine.

Permission is granted to duplicate this page for local church use only. © 2013 Abingdon Press.

Memory Verse Puzzle

5c

"The light shines in the darkness, and the darkness doesn't extinguish the light."
—John 1:5

Praise God! Jesus Is Born!

by LeeDell Stickler and Judy Newman-St. John

(Trumpet sounds) Give ear! Give ear! By order of the Emperor Augustus, all men will go to their hometowns to be registered. **(Trumpet sounds)**

And so Joseph went from Nazareth in Galilee to Judea, to the city of David called Bethlehem, because he was from the house and family of David. And he took with him Mary, who was expecting a child.

(Donkey hooves) Up the hills and down the hills, the little donkey walked. **(Donkey hooves)** The sun was going down. Soon it would be night.

(Donkey hooves) Mary was tired. Joseph was tired. And the little donkey was even more tired. **(Donkey hooves)**

When the three came to the little town of Bethlehem, there was quite a crowd. **(Crowd sounds)** In fact the city was so crowded that there was no place to stay.

Joseph went from house to house. **(Donkey hooves)** He was looking for some place—any place—to stay where Mary could rest and have shelter. There was not an inch of floor space to be found anywhere. Finally Joseph came to an inn. **(Door sounds)** The innkeeper opened the door. **(Crowd sounds)**

"Go away!" said the innkeeper. "We have no room tonight!" Joseph turned to go, pulling the little donkey behind him. **(Donkey hooves)** The innkeeper saw Mary and the tired little donkey. He felt sorry for them.

"Wait. I have no room inside the inn, but I do have a stable where travelers keep their animals. You may sleep there tonight if you'd like," he said.

Joseph looked at Mary wondering how she would feel about sleeping where the animals slept. Mary looked at Joseph and nodded her head yes. Joseph turned back to the innkeeper and nodded.

"Let me show you the way," the kind innkeeper offered. "The stable is just over here." The innkeeper led Joseph and Mary and the little donkey to the small stable. **(Donkey hooves)**

The three looked around. It wasn't much, but there would be a roof over them tonight. And the animals would keep them company. **(Animal sounds)**

Joseph led the little donkey to hay to eat and water to drink. **(Donkey hooves)** Then he took the bundles from the donkey's back and put them close to Mary.

And that night, that very night, with only Joseph and the animals to keep her company, **(soft animal sounds)** Mary gave birth to baby Jesus. She wrapped him in bands of cloth and laid him in the manger where the animals ate.

In that region there were shepherds in the fields, keeping watch over their flock. The angel of the Lord appeared to them and told them good news of great joy. **(Chorus: Praise God! Jesus is born!)**

The angel told the shepherds they would find the child lying in a manger. **(Chorus: Praise God! Jesus is born!)**

The shepherds hurried and found the child in the stable, just as the angel had told them. They told everyone about the child. **(Chorus: Praise God! Jesus is born!)**

The shepherds returned to the field glorifying and praising God for all they had seen and heard. **(Chorus: Praise God! Jesus is born!)** **(Chorus: Praise God! Jesus is born!)** **(Chorus: Praise God! Jesus is born!)**

Permission is granted to duplicate this page for local church use only. © 2013 Abingdon Press.